THE Beet Fields

GARY PAULSEN

RED FOX DEFiniTiONS

This one's for Gito

AUTHOR'S NOTE

I have been telling stories for many years, mining my life for the ore that makes each piece of fiction, as most writers mine their lives for material to make stories come to life and dance.

Because of that, small portions of this book appeared in softer forms, shadowed and sketched and changed into gentler fiction, over twenty years ago. But here it is now as real as I can write it, and as real as I can remember it happening. It is strange what one remembers:

Light through a dusty little trailer window, the smell of an unfiltered cigarette, the shine of metal on a hoe working in a beet field, the sweat on a forearm, the pop of a tractor motor, the soft hair at a farm girl's temples when she pays for a ride at the fair — all of these came to me when I started to work on this book, all these true things came and let me see more things honestly, to help me lift those parts of stories back out of fiction and into the real story of what happened in that summer of the beet fields ...

Shee gave me of the Tree, and I did eate.

John Milton, *Paradise Lost*

1955. The boy's life truly began when he was sixteen years old, sleeping in the grubby apartment, in his small room, on the couch that folded out into a bed. He was only half awake, fighting sleep: half dreaming, half knowing. His mother was there beside him.

She had come to his bed many times drunk, to sleep, as she had slept with him when he was a small boy during the war, when his father was away in the army. She was the mother and he was the boy and they lived alone. All his life she had fallen asleep near him, two, three nights a week, and he would either slide to the side away from her or ease out onto the floor and pull a blanket down to sleep there while she passed out, mumbling drunkenly about his father. Always about the father.

But tonight, even half dreaming, he knew something was different, wrong, about her need for him, and he rolled and pushed and stood away in lonely horror while she lay there moaning, half conscious, the drunk smell of her filling his shabby room, dark except for the light from a streetlamp a block away. And he ran ...

ONE

The North Dakota sun came up late.

They were already in the beet fields and had taken up their hoes with the handles cut off so they could not be leaned upon to rest; had already eaten cold beans and slices of week-old bread from the metal pie pans nailed to the table to be hosed off between shifts of eaters; had already filled themselves on rusty water from the two-handled milk cans on the wagon at the end of the field; had already peed and taken a dump and scratched and spat and splashed cold water in their faces to drip down their necks.

Had done all of these after sleeping the short night on feed sacks in sleeping sheds near the barn; after they had come into a new day, *then* the sun came up.

The Mexicans always outworked him. They spread out at the south end of the sugar-beet fields and began to work, and the Mexicans always outworked him. At first he tried to understand how that could be. It was all so simple. They were to walk down the rows of beets and remove every other beet. The farmers – he always thought of them as the farmers – planted more seeds than they needed, to ensure proper germination, and the seeds all came up and had to be thinned to allow the beets to grow properly.

So they worked down the rows, cutting left and right, taking a beet, leaving a beet, and it did not seem possible that one person could do it that much faster than another, but always the Mexican men and women, and even children, outworked him. Even when he worked hard, hacked back and forth without looking, worked in a frenzy until his hands bled on the handle, he could not keep up. Their white shirts always drifted ahead of him, farther and farther out like white birds flying low, until they were so far ahead they were spots and then nothing.

Rows of beets a mile long. Left and right for a mile and then turn and start back, halfway up to meet the Mexicans coming back.

Eleven dollars an acre. Four rows to the acre, a half acre a day, all day the hoes cutting, left and right, the rows never ending, and even trying to catch up with the Mexicans was not enough to stop the boredom, nothing to stop the awful boredom of the beets.

The sun was hot when it came up late. There was no early-morning coolness, no relief. An early heat came with the first edge of the sun and by the time the sun was full up, he was cooking and looking for some relief.

He tried hoeing with his left hand low, then his right hand, then leaning forward more, then less, but nothing helped. It was hot, getting hotter, and he straightened and spat and resettled the straw hat he had bought in Grafton. It had a piece of green plastic in the brim that looked cool but wasn't. He had bought the hat because all the Mexicans had them and he wanted to look like them, blend in with them in the field even though they were a rich dark colour and he looked like white paper burned around the edges. But the hat did not seem to fit right and he kept readjusting it to get the sweatband broken in.

It was the same with his hands. They did not break in. He had been working three days now, but blisters had rebroken and left pink skin that opened and bled. He bought leather gloves from the farmer who sold them the hoes. The farmer sold them hoes for three dollars and gloves for another two dollars and they had to pay a dollar a day for a sandwich and he had worked three days and had only hoed an acre. Not counting the hat, which he'd bought with money he'd found in his pockets when he ran, he had now earned eleven dollars, with three taken out for the hoe and three for sandwiches and two for the gloves and four and a half for three dinners, and fifty cents a night for three nights. After three days' work, he owed the farmer three dollars. He did the maths while he worked.

'I pay eleven dollars an acre,' the farmer had told him. 'You can hoe an acre a day easy – eleven dollars a day.'

When he'd started hoeing he dreamed of wealth, did the maths constantly until the numbers filled his mind. Eleven dollars an acre, an acre a day; after ten days a hundred and ten dollars, twenty days the almost-unheard-of sum of two hundred and twenty dollars. More than a man made per month working in a factory for a dollar an hour – and he was only sixteen. Rich. He would be rich.

But after the first day when his back would not straighten and his hands would not uncurl from the hoe handle and his blisters were bleeding, after all that and two-fifty for food, and three for the hoe, and fifty cents for the lodging, not to mention the hat and gloves, only a third of an acre had been thinned that first day, and he knew he would not get rich, would never be rich. By the second day he was no longer even sad about not being rich and laughed with the Mexicans who would also never be rich but who smiled and laughed all the time while they worked. Now, on the fourth day, gloved, he just hoed.

He worked hard, his head down, the hoe snaking left and right. An hour could have passed, a minute, a day, a year. He did not look up, kept working until it seemed it should be time for a break, and he stood and looked across the field to the north where the Mexicans were small white dots, moving farther ahead as he watched.

'Shit.' Swearing helped. His back ached and it wasn't yet midday and he was thirsty, his tongue stuck to the sides of his mouth with the dryness, but the milk cans of water in the old pickup were a half mile behind him and he didn't want to take the time to walk back for a drink. They would bring water at midday along with the dry sand-wiches, when the sun was nearly overhead. Another hour to go. 'Shit.'

Before bending back to the hoe – the 'fuuwaucking hoe', as the old Mexican who led the group called it – he looked around the field, closely first at individual beet plants, then out until they blurred in green, and then farther out, around and out and up, in all directions. It was like standing in the centre of an enormous bowl that went green to the sky and then yellow blue into the gold-hot sun, the colour mixing with the heat in some way to press down on him, pressing, pushing, bending, driving him back to the hoe.

He cut left and right; cut and cut, the beet plants flipping off the shiny blade of the hoe, working again without looking up, giving himself to the beets until his back was hot with the sun overhead and he heard the grinding of a motor coming along the side of the field, and he looked up to see the farmer's wife bringing food.

She was a thin woman, and she had a revolver on the seat of the truck, next to her, blue steel with a short barrel. There were bullets in the revolver. He had seen the small rounded ends shining from the cylinder. She knew how to use the gun; he had heard her talking to her husband.

'I don't want no Mexicans after my body,' she'd said. 'They come after my body and I'm going to shoot them and I know how to do it, too. I don't give a darn about no Mexicans and no nasty beets, neither.'

The farmer had nodded but looked embarrassed at the same time and he ate apart from the Mexicans, and the boy thought it must be because he was embarrassed about the gun but it might be because he got good food, thick sandwiches with meat and coffee, and the people working the hoes got week-old garbage for food.

He thought it was all meaningless because the farmer's wife was nowhere near as pretty as some of the Mexican women, who had thick black hair and dark eyes that lifted at the corner. Their bodies were full and rich, where the farmer's wife looked rail-skinny and empty; none of the Mexican men looked at her but always away and to the side.

But she kept the gun close to her side when she came with the sandwiches. The Mexicans did not seem to mind the gun, or at least said nothing about it even when they were alone in the barn making beds with the feed sacks – unless they said it in Spanish, which he did not understand. Usually they spoke in English when he was around, except to tease each other and sometimes him, and he thought that Mexico must be a very fine place because they were always laughing and joking and didn't pay any attention to the gun.

The dollar sandwiches were made of week-old bread with a thin layer of peanut butter without any jelly. He would not have eaten one but he was so hungry he could not stand to not eat. Even with the sandwiches he was hungry; the afternoon would go on for ever if he didn't eat.

There was a huge pile of the sandwiches on the plate set out on the hood, open to flies and bugs, and the farmer's wife was happy to hand them out – always with the gun close by, of course – and she made a small mark on a piece of paper for each sandwich. Each mark a dollar against the money for hoeing beets. But he was the only one to take a sandwich.

The Mexicans came from the field, somehow always so clean that their white clothes made his eyes hurt. They had corn-tortilla burritos with beans in them and the boy envied them the beans and tortillas but was too shy to ask for one.

Each night near the sleeping sheds, the Mexicans cooked a large pot of pinto beans, except they called them *frijoles*. The pot was cast iron and big enough to cook five pounds of beans at a time. While the beans were cooking the men took turns finding bits of wood along the fencerows and in the brushy ditches to burn under the pot and the women put a piece of metal over another part of the fire and made tortillas with a sound that made the boy think of music.

They would take a small blob of dough from a bowl and use their hands in a slapping motion for rhythm, *slap-push-slap-push*, while they talked to each other, and somehow they did not seem tired from the fields the way he felt tired each night.

Six, eight slaps and a small corn tortilla would fly out of their hands, fly like a round golden bird and land on the red-hot metal to hiss once and then fry, giving off a smell that seemed to come from the earth and from corn and from all the food the boy had ever eaten. One woman to make the tortillas and flick them onto the hot metal and another woman to use her finger and thumb and, as deft as any doctor, catch an edge of each tortilla and flip it. A flip so quick it made the tortilla dance, up and over and down on the new side to cook, and then, in seconds, off to be wrapped in a clean piece of cloth near the fire, where there was a stack of them, thin and tall and smelling of heaven.

During the day the men found the things to put in the beans. The boy did not always see what they found. Sometimes a root or other vegetable, now and then squirrels, which they killed with little leather slings and round rocks, once a rabbit, and twice some woodchucks that lived in holes along a fencerow and came out to *chukker* a warning when they went by. The woodchucks and rabbit they took out of their holes with a long piece of old barbed wire shaped like a crank on one end. They stuck the wire down in the hole and twisted the crank end until the barbed wire wrapped up in the animal's fur and then they jerked it out and killed it with a hoe, all done very quickly so they wouldn't lose time thinning the beets.

All the men carried knives, sharp and clean, and some of them had switchblades. The boy had seen switchblades before but the Mexican men used them more correctly in some way, so that when they took a knife from their loose trousers and either snapped or flicked the blade open it seemed to become part of their hands while they neatly gutted and skinned the animal and wrapped the meat in a piece of sacking.

Whatever else they put in the beans, the women always added some garlic and spices and red chillis, which they carried on a string, and the smell that came from the pot when they opened the lid to add the small animals or to stir the beans with a large wooden spoon while the steam worked out into the air, *that* smell was almost impossible for the boy to endure.

But he was shy and did not dare ask for the food even when he was standing in the hot sun paying a dollar for a sandwich that was covered with fly specks and tasted like crap handed to him by a woman with a .38 lying on the seat beside her.

As on the previous three days, the Mexicans moved off by themselves to sit and eat and the boy took his sandwich and sat away to the side and ate it in four dry bites, just getting it out of the way. The sandwich was only enough to make him more hungry and he lay back on the warm grass and fought buying another one because it would put him behind in wages and the thought of working this hard for a dry sandwich was insane.

'Here, eat this.'

The boy opened his eyes to see the oldest Mexican man, over forty, holding out two tortillas wrapped around cold beans. For a second the boy stared. He had been with them three and a half days now and none of them had said a word to him.

'I haven't got any money.'

The man drew back, his eyes hard. 'It is not for money. For money I would let your skinny ass die. It is because you do not have any meat on your bones and you are young.' He held out the burritos again. 'Eat these.'

The boy reached for them. 'I'm sorry. I'm new at all this. Thank you.'

'You are new at everything. It is because you are young.' The Mexican turned back to the others and said something in Spanish the boy did not understand and all the Mexicans laughed. But it was not mean laughter, and besides, the smell of the burritos stuffed with beans was overpowering.

He ate them in a few bites, swallowing the pieces whole, and his stomach growled and it was all done before the old Mexican had turned to leave.

The man said something in Spanish to the group and they all laughed again and then he turned to the boy. 'You are like a wolf or a village dog. You eat quickly.'

'They were so good I couldn't help myself.' The boy smiled. 'I've been watching how you cook and eat and it makes me more hungry and the slop they feed us at night is awful.' Each night the farmer's wife brought out a big pan full of shredded potatoes fried in lard — burned in lard would be more accurate — and more of the week-old bread, and this was to be eaten with no salt or pepper from plates nailed to a picnic table with a roofing nail through the centre of each. 'Awful,' he repeated. And for this he was supposed to pay another dollar-fifty.

'Perhaps you should eat with us at night as well.'

'I ... don't have anything. You all put something in the pot and I don't have anything.'

The man nodded. 'I see. That is a problem, is it not?' He thought for a moment, exaggerating it by rubbing the stubble on his chin with his hand. 'Perhaps there is a solution. Can you climb?'

'Pardon?'

'Climb — can you climb? We do not like to climb.'

The boy shrugged. 'I guess I can, why?'

'There is a large flock of pigeons that come to the farm — perhaps you have seen them?'

The boy nodded. 'They fly around the barn. There must be hundreds of them.'

'Ah, yes. Those very ones. The *patrón*' — he spat

out the word – 'does not like the pigeons. He says they cover everything with their *guduo*. But pigeons are good to eat. So this works for both of us. The *patrón* wants the birds gone and we wish to eat them. The pigeons can easily be captured when they roost and sleep in the evenings. The difficulty lies in where they sleep. It is in the barn's rafters and we do not like to climb.'

The boy nodded again. 'You want me to climb up there and get some pigeons tonight.'

'*Exactamente*. We are afraid of climbing but the pigeons are made of such delicate meat ...'

The boy was sure he was lying. If they wanted the pigeons they would get them, just as they hoed beets, get them better than he could, probably faster and better. They were just trying to be nice and letting him feel that he was contributing to the pot.

'Sure,' he said. 'I'll do it.'

And then it was time to hoe again, working through the sun of the afternoon, always trying to catch them and not seeing them again until the Mexicans had turned at the end of the field and started back to meet him.

They hoed until just before dark when it was time to stand – the boy took for ever to unbend and straighten – and walk to the house and barn and shed where everyone slept.

This time the boy walked more with the group and felt some of the shyness leave and though they talked in Spanish they did not seem to mind him walking there and two of the young ones, boys not ten years old – who also outworked him – dropped back to walk with him. They were wearing those strikingly white men's dress shirts, which were too large for them, and the tan of their skin looked rich next to the white cloth and he wondered why all the men where he came from called them such dark names when their skin was really so beautiful. He had seen almost no Mexicans until now.

He loved to hear these people talk, the words ending in questions, moving up to make music, and the women's voices fitting into the men's so it almost became a song.

As they approached the yard they stopped talking.

The farmer's woman was at the wooden table with her large pot of lard-fried shredded potatoes. She smiled a thin smile when they walked by and some of the Mexicans smiled back but many looked away, and the boy did as well. He had been the only one to eat at the table last night and tonight he would eat with the Mexicans and the woman with the gun could blow it out her skinny ass. That was how he thought of it literally, blowing something out her ass except that he added the word *skinny* – blow it out her skinny ass.

The Mexicans went to the sleeping shed and started chores. Some started the fire under the beans. Two men went with a basin to a water barrel and came back with water to wash and all the men and women washed their hands and dried them on a feed sack hanging from the wall. Two women put the piece of metal for tortillas on the flames and started working dough in a bowl next to the fire while the metal became hot.

The boy waited until they were done and the older man motioned to him and he washed his hands as well.

'We will eat first,' the man said, smiling, his teeth even and white. 'And then we shall see to the pigeons.'

When the farmer's wife saw that the boy was not coming to eat the potatoes and dry bread she took the pot back in the house and the old Mexican laughed.

'She will make her husband eat that. He won't crap for a week.'

There was a large stack of tortillas in the cloth wrapping and the Mexicans formed a line, the old man taking the boy with him. As each person came to the cookfire a woman there took two tortillas, ladled beans into them, expertly rolled them into burritos and handed them up from the fire.

The garlic smell had the boy salivating long before he came to the fire and when he took the tortillas and thanked the woman she laughed and said something in Spanish he did not understand and pinched the flesh on his ribs.

'She says you are too skinny to love,' the old man told him. 'She does not mean love as a mother loves.'

The boy blushed and thought of his mother and the blush grew worse and he mumbled something and moved to the side of the shed under the eaves to eat the hot burritos. He thought he had never eaten anything so delicious, even Thanksgiving dinners at his grandmother's when she cooked like they had on the farms when she was young and there was so much food the table sagged. He compared many things to her Thanksgiving dinners. Not just food but other parts of his life as well, parts before he had to run. He had bought a new Hiawatha bicycle with a chrome tank and horn and with spring shock absorbers on the front, and he thought of the bicycle in comparison to that meal — that the bicycle was as good a bike as the meal was good food or that his Savage .410 single-shot shotgun that he'd bought by setting pins by Ray's bowling alley was as good a shotgun as that meal.

Of course, all that was behind him now. He'd left the bike and the gun and a box of treasures he'd found and saved over the years when he'd gone off to find a new life for himself – and those were all things of his childhood. Now, he thought he had only to work and be a man, although he missed the shotgun and the bicycle and some of the treasures, like the arrowhead buried in a piece of bone that he thought was a human leg bone but wasn't sure. Even that was gone in his new life, and now what he had to compare to Thanksgiving dinners were the beans and tortillas, and he felt they were the most wonderful thing of all, even when he was done and leaning back against the side of the shed.

The old man came to him and offered him a sack of Bull Durham tobacco with wheat-straw papers on the side.

'Thank you.' He rolled a cigarette clumsily. He'd learned to smoke in the bowling alley and had been inhaling for over a year, since he was fifteen, but he was accustomed to tailor-mades and hadn't rolled many Bull Durhams. The paper had no glue and had to be licked several times before it stuck, and when he lit the cigarette with a match the man gave him and dragged deeply, nearly the whole cigarette burned up. He inhaled and held it, ashamed to be coughing slightly, and nodded. 'It's good.' It was harsh and hot and seemed to tear his lungs apart, but he didn't want to appear ungrateful. 'Tastes good.'

The old man hesitated, then sighed. 'I must ask you a difficult question before we take up the matter of the pigeons.'

'What is it?'

'You understand I would not ask such a question except that it is important to us.'

'What is the question?'

'Do the police look for you?'

'The police?'

'I know, I know. One does not ask it lightly. But we came across the border in the night and rode the night buses to get here. If the police are searching for you they may find us as well and give us some trouble. That is why I ask. To avoid the trouble.'

'Oh.'

'Do they? Do the police look for you?'

'I don't know. I didn't do anything wrong except run off …'

'You left your family?'

He did not think of them as a family. They were a man who drank until he pissed his pants and people saw him walking down the street with piss running down his leg and puke on his shirt and laughed; and a woman who lived in the bottle and had tried to do the thing – the thing – to him in the darkened room. He could not, would not, think of them as a family. 'I just left, is all. Ran off.'

'Will your mother and father not look for you?'

He shook his head. 'I don't think so. I don't know.'

'Ah. So it is best if we watch for a time.'

'They would not know where to look, where I've gone.'

'Just the same, if they tell the police that you have run off, they may think of looking for you here or there. So we will prepare ourselves.'

'I'm sorry.'

The old Mexican shrugged. 'Many times the police don't bother even when they see us. It is only that we must be ready.'

'I could leave.'

'Yes, there is that. But they might look wherever it is you go as well as here – you might as well stay. And too, if you go, what do we do for the pigeons?'

The boy smiled. 'I forgot about that.'

It was dark and the beans had settled in for the night and the boy wanted to sleep more than anything, wanted to hide from the day's hoeing in sleep, but the old man led him into the barn.

'They are up there,' he whispered.

The barn was really more of an equipment

storage shed, an enormous metal-roofed building with latticed-steel curved girders to hold the roof up and looked more like a hangar than a barn.

At the peak the rafters were an easy thirty-five feet off the dirt floor and it was there, where the girders curved over the top, that the pigeons roosted. They flew in the open doors on either end of the building in the evening and settled in the top curve of the roof for the night.

The boy moved to the side of the building where the girders came down to the ground. He could not see up into the peak but the girder curved up and away, and he took hold through the struts and started to climb. He'd loved to climb trees when he was younger and was quick and light, and at first it was easy climbing. But soon the girder curved overhead and he was climbing virtually upside down and finally he stopped, hanging amid the sleeping pigeons. He let go for an instant and reached for one of the pigeons and tried to catch it but slapped at it instead and it fluttered away in the dark.

'It is necessary for the pigeons to die for us to have the meat,' the old man prompted. 'You must release your hold with one hand and contain the pigeon.'

By now the boy was hanging with his arms and legs poked through the girder. He could let go with one hand and hang on with the other and one knee, but only just, and as soon as he let go his body seemed to want to fall.

'I can't do it,' he called down.

'Ah, well, if you can't you can't.'

The disappointment in the man's voice seemed to rise in the dark barn and it became more important than ever for the boy to catch the pigeons. He took a breath, heard a pigeon cooing on the rafter over his head, and he let go of the girder with his right hand and snatched the bird from its roost.

He caught the pigeon by one leg. As soon as he grabbed it the pigeon began flapping, trying to get away and becoming more frantic as it fought, panicking the boy, who hung onto the bird with one hand and realized that he would be hard-pressed to simply stay in the rafters, let alone do anything with the bird.

The old Mexican seemed to read his mind. 'For the bird to drop to me you must kill it first. Wring the neck. Otherwise it will fly away.'

'I can't—'

'Ah, well, then, if you can't you can't.'

Somehow the boy clawed the pigeon back up to the rafter, shoved his arm through a hole in the girder, hung by his elbow and snatched at the bird's head with his hand. On the fourth try he caught it, twisted it hard and jerked and felt blood and pigeon shit fall in his face and mouth. He dropped the dead bird, sputtering, 'Shit!'

'I have the bird,' the old man called up. 'It is a fine bird, plump and round from all the grain it finds here.'

'I'm coming down.'

'But there are many mouths. One bird will not go very far. Surely since you are up there already you might stay a while and get more birds. See how they become calm, waiting for you?'

And he was right. When the boy had grabbed the pigeon the rest of them had fluttered and moved over on the rafters, but as soon as he dropped the dead one they settled and went back to sleep. He moved a bit on the rafters and grabbed another one.

This time it went much better. He caught the bird by the body so it couldn't flutter and disturb the rest, hung by his elbow and one knee through the girder, broke the neck and dropped it all in one motion.

'Good,' the old man said. 'That one was dead as it hit my hand.'

Then another, cleaner this time, the first feel of the warm bird in his hand when he snatched it from the rafter, two, three quick heartbeats and then the snap of the neck and the bird dropped;

then another, and he was into a rhythm now. Swinging with his arms and legs hooked through the rafters, grabbing a pigeon and snap-wringing the head until the pigeon flapped in death, and then down, to drop to the waiting old man below.

'Excellent,' the old man said. 'You are of an excellent nature at this—'

It was here that the boy fell.

He became sure of himself, too sure, was thinking, Hell, I'll take them all, every pigeon up here, take them and feed the whole group. They'll all eat meat tonight and then the girl, he thought, the girl who had walked near him and smiled with white teeth, that girl will think—

He never decided what she would think. Just as the word came into his mind his hands came loose and his leg straightened and he dropped, plummeted, holding a pigeon in his hand, fell like a stone until he landed flat on his back, on the dirt floor, and there was a splash of some colour in his brain that he couldn't remember later and then nothing. Not pain, not sound, not a thing. Nothing.

TWO

Light.

There was lightness, seen from the inside of a cloud, white light that came from all directions, somehow came from inside him as well as out, and he opened his eyes.

The white light did not go away, grew more intense with his eyes open.

'Can you feel this?' Somebody pinched his legs and it hurt. He swore.

'That is good. Move something now, move this foot …'

The boy started to focus and saw that what he thought was white light was really the shirt of the old man reflecting the glare from the bulb hanging in the shed where they slept.

He moved his foot, then his hands and arms, each as he was told to move, and at last his neck. By now an older woman – at least forty – was there and she said something in Spanish and felt his neck and shoulders, then smiled at him with even white teeth and said something more.

'She says you are young and green and did not break,' the old man said. 'I thought surely a bone or two would have snapped. You fell such a distance,' he laughed, 'and even when you were senseless you did not let go of the pigeon.' He smiled. 'You must be a true hunter.'

Which made the boy feel proud because he had hunted, had thrown himself at the woods to escape the drinking and fancied himself a good hunter. 'I hurt.'

'As you should. The ground shook when you fell. But it will be worse tomorrow when you awaken – you must sleep now.'

The boy rolled onto his side and then rose to his knees. He did not want to appear weak in front of the old man or the woman kneeling next to him or the two girls standing off to the side, so he stood, wobbling, and made his way to his sleeping area and fell onto his bed of feed sacks and was asleep, or unconscious again, instantly.

In the morning he thought, I am paralysed. He had slept on his right side, a rolled-up feed sack for a pillow, and he had drooled and his head was pressed into the wetness. He wanted to move it away but he could not.

His body screamed with pain. Every bone, every muscle, his head, even his teeth, ached and when at last he made something move – he swung his leg sideways – it was pure agony.

He rolled slowly onto his back and opened his eyes. There was daylight, bright sun, cutting into the gloom of the shed and he knew that he was very late – it must be close to nine - and that all the Mexicans were gone to the fields and would get so far ahead of him he would never catch up. In his life he would never catch up, he thought, and then he saw the farmer's wife come in the door.

His sleeping area was way in the back of the shed, tucked in a dark corner so that somebody coming in from the bright sun would not be able to see to the rear where he lay. He held his breath, watching her, wondering.

She wore a loose red–print dress that hung on her like a drape. She stopped at the first bed on the left side – the men slept on the left, the women on the right – and reached down to pull a sack up from the floor. She held the sack in her left hand and put it to her face, her cheek, and then to her nose and smelled it and breathed the odour of the sack and at the same time she slid her other hand down her body.

The boy forgot the pain and felt himself grow hard and at the same time confused because she had said she hated the Mexicans and didn't want the men to get her and yet here she was breathing in the smell of them.

He knew that if she saw him now she would probably go and get the pistol and shoot him but he needn't have worried. In a moment she re-arranged the sack as it had been, straightened her dress, turned and walked out of the shed, and he lay back to ponder what he had seen. The pain had returned and he thought he might just lie there all day thinking of the skinny farmer's wife and what she had done but he had to pee so badly that he finally stood, moaning from the pain, and made his way to the outhouse behind the shed.

Once he was up and moving, the pain seemed to lessen and after using the outhouse he slowly walked the half mile out to the field and picked up his hoe where the Mexicans had left it and went to work, carefully, cutting left and right, left and right, every other beet.

When at last it was time for lunch he sat with the men and ate tortillas with beans and after they had eaten he told the old man what he had seen in the sleeping shed that morning.

The man laughed and turned and said something in Spanish to the other men and then looked to where the farmer's wife sat in the truck, a hundred yards away. She had brought sandwiches, though nobody was eating them now, and sat in the cab of the pickup with the gun next to her.

'She does not know herself,' the old man said, the smile leaving his face. 'Her husband must not be much of a man and she feels the moon on her shoulder and wants but cannot have and so does not know herself.'

'What does that mean?' The boy wiped his hands on his jeans. 'The moon on her shoulder, what is that?'

'It is something we say in the village where I come from. Women are said to have the moon on their shoulder when they are not satisfied.' He sighed and looked up at the noon sun. 'It is said that men have the most lust but women have more – they have all the lust. They want everything. Marta, hey, Marta,' he called to the older Mexican woman. 'Marta – do you have lust?'

The woman was lying against a grassy bank on the fencerow along the edge of the field with her hat over her eyes and she raised the hat. *'I Qué?'*

He said something in Spanish. The woman laughed and gave the old man the finger and then went back to resting.

'But it is true,' the man said. 'Women have all the lust there is. They are never satisfied. They all have the moon on their shoulder.'

The boy lay back, half asleep, smiling, thinking of it until they went back to the hoes. Working through the afternoon burned the pain and stiffness off and by quitting time he was back to normal and starving.

Somebody had cleaned the pigeons the night before and put them in a shady corner of the shed, in a pot with cool water, covered to keep the flies out.

Soon they had the fire going and when the beans were cooked, after dark, the pigeons were put in and some dried chillis, and the stew simmered while the boy sat dozing in the corner and the Mexicans talked. He listened to the music of their talk instead of the words.

Finally the food was ready and the women cooked tortillas and everybody ate until they were full, standing around the pot, picking the pigeon meat of the bones and wrapping it with beans in the tortillas.

The boy thought it must be near midnight when they were done and full and had smoked rolled cigarettes and still the men sat and talked in one place while the women talked in another.

He could hardly keep his eyes open and moved to his sleeping area but the old man came over to him.

'Are we not to get more pigeons?'

'Tonight?'

'It is when they sleep.'

'But it's late.' The boy never wanted to climb again. 'And we have to work tomorrow.'

'Not tomorrow. It is *domingo* – Sunday. We do

not work on this day.'

'But—'

'Did you not like the pigeons?'

More than like, the boy thought, his belly full and the pigeon fat still on his lips with the faint burn from the chilli — much more than like. 'Yes.'

'Is it that you are afraid to climb again? That would show an understanding — if you were afraid to climb. A fall like that would cause an under-standing of the risk …'

It was important that a man not be afraid and so the boy felt concerned. Later he would wonder, when he was no longer with the Mexicans, if the old man had done it intentionally to make him face his fear or, perhaps, just because he wanted more pigeons.

Whatever the intent, the result was the same. With a full belly and fear in his heart the boy went to the equipment barn and climbed upside down to the rafters for more pigeons.

The fear helped rather than hindered him, made him cautious and slow and kept him from falling. He climbed and dropped the pigeons one after another until finally the old man called up, 'It is enough. We have enough to eat and more will only spoil.'

The boy climbed down and was ready for bed but it was not to be, not yet. They went to the sleeping shed and sat at the back with the glow from the bulb hanging inside and cleaned the pigeons, everybody helping, men and women, ripping the skins from the birds and thumbing the guts out expertly while the old man told them the story of getting the pigeons, first in English for the boy and then in Spanish for the rest.

'He went through the birds like a bad wind,' the old man said, 'holding as sure as would a panther, killing left and killing right until I made him stop. It was a thing to see.'

And the boy knew that he was being half teased, but still, there were the birds being cleaned and they would eat the next day because he had climbed the rafters and dropped the dead birds down. It made him conscious of the way the women looked at him – or how he imagined they looked at him – and when at last the long aching day was done and he crawled onto his feed sacks near dawn to sleep, he could not help feeling pride that he had killed the pigeons.

THREE

The days bled one into another and the work fed on itself until he could not distinguish a change. He measured time in happenings, not days or weeks.

There was the day of the snake. He was working next to a small girl of eight or nine or ten, he could not tell. Somehow a rattlesnake had found its way this far north and into the beets. The girl was hoeing and the boy saw the snake and while he had never seen one before, he knew instantly what it was and he froze. The snake was two feet from his right leg and he could do nothing, but the girl simply reached across two rows with her hoe and with an almost delicate flick took the snake's head off. All without looking up, without pausing, with no acknowledgement that the boy existed, she killed the snake and moved on, missed one beet strike to kill a snake, then on, the small girl with the straw hat on her head moving off down the row while he stood, still frozen, watching the snake roll over and over, its pale belly writhing as its nerves slowly died.

And the day of the Madonna. There was a

woman he did not know by name – he thought Maria but several of them were named Maria – and he thought she should not be there because she was enormous with child. He had seen pregnant aunts and some cousins and women on the street back in town but none this large. She was of course beautiful, as he thought all the Mexican women were, with thick black hair and dark almond eyes and skin the colour of caramel and the pregnancy made her more beautiful in some way he did not understand. He felt it was wrong for her to work in the field. There came a day when he was not twenty feet away from her and she was bent hoeing and she swore, '*I Chinga!*' Then he heard the sound of liquid splashing and saw water running down her legs beneath her skirt and she looked at the boy, through the boy at something he could not imagine, and went down to her knees and then onto her back.

The boy screamed at the men and they saw her go down and came running, one of them her husband or the man the boy thought was her husband, and the boy moved closer to help, though he had no idea what to do.

In the end, there wasn't much for him to do. It was not her first pregnancy and she heaved some and lay back and heaved some more with two younger women helping her and on the fourth heave or maybe the fortieth – the boy had never seen such pain on anyone's face – a baby slid out, onto one of the men's shirts, to be caught by the women who were helping her. They wiped the baby with another shirt and handed it to the woman and one of the younger women said the words *Santa Maria* very softly and here the new mother did a strange thing.

She put the baby on her breasts and covered it with her hands so that the palms were over the baby's eyes and she dug her heels in and tried to push away, hiding the baby, and the boy felt she was embarrassed because he had watched all of it and thought she did not want him to see.

'She is hiding the baby from us,' he said, looking away. 'From me.'

'No,' the old man said. 'Not you. She is hiding the baby from the beets so that they will not see him and in that way perhaps he'll never have to know the beets.'

So he learned that they hated the beets as he did, and he marvelled all the more at their humour, which was always there, and their grace.

And so another week passed.

There came a day when he could bend to the hoe and chop in a rhythm that held a kind of grace and at the end of that day he looked up and saw that he had matched the work of his Mexican companions.

Soon after, they ran out of beets and they had to leave. But there were many farmers with beets to thin and they simply walked down the road a mile and started another endless field with rows that went up to the sky and its hot sun and that gave them the ache-joy of work and new pots of beans and meat and tortillas to eat.

The boy did not know how long it would last, did not care, but centred on the work and the Mexicans as he would have centred on a family if he'd had a family; if he thought of how it might all come to end he assumed he would just go on with them.

One night the old man sat and smoked and told him of working in California in the fruit orchards and picking lettuce and artichokes and the boy nodded.

He had money now. He had his hoe and gloves and had come up to an acre a day, and kept it all except for ten cents every four days for Bull Durham tobacco and papers, which the farmer bought for a nickel and sold to them for a dime. His pockets were jammed with money because he rarely went to town and spent it, except for one brief trip to replace his tattered jeans. He had adopted the fears of the Mexicans as well as their work habits.

'Everybody knows we are here,' the old man told him on another evening. 'They know we are not legal; we are like ghosts that they see but do not recognize. As long as we just work and do not go into town or make a difficulty we are all right and they leave us alone.'

And so the boy decided it would be the same for him. He would just work and pocket the money and not make a difficulty and he did not think past it.

The next farm only kept them busy for eight days and then on to the next, where the boy fell in love.

He had of course been in love many times with different girls in school, an aching love, a love of blue eyes and ponytails and bobby sox and pointy new brassieres and teasing laughter and red lips and furtive looks – a love that brought pain from the centre of his life. The girls didn't see him. None of the girls knew him or thought of him because he was not popular and did not play sports or dress right and had drunks for parents. But he loved them still; loved them with all that he was, loved Shirley and Anne and Elaine and had dreams of them until his life was ruined and he ran off.

He had decided that he would go through life poor and with a broken heart – well, less poor now that he was making good money hoeing beets.

Then they came to the Bill Flaherty farm.

It was almost time to stop thinning beets in North Dakota because the plants had grown too large and other illegal workers had worked other fields and there were none left. The old man had talked to the boy again of riding a bus out to California to work the fields there when in some way – the boy never understood how the Mexicans came to know things – word came that there was another local farm that needed beets thinned.

They walked four miles down a dirt road, wearing their straw hats with the green plastic brims and carrying their clothes and belongings in feed sacks – the boy now had two pairs of Levi's, an extra pair of tennis shoes and a light windbreaker and two T-shirts, plus his hoe and gloves to carry – until they saw a sign scrawled with black paint on cardboard that said:

THINNERS NEEDED

And they turned in to see an eighty-acre field of beets.

Eighty acres was not much; they had worked fields that were so long they could not see the far end when they started, giant farms, and this small stand would not take them a week working at their normal rate.

So the old man went to the house while they waited and soon a short barrel-chested man wearing an old felt hat came out and looked at them. He smiled and spat a brown stream of tobacco juice and said to the boy, 'How the hell did *you* get in with these people?'

'I work with them.'

The man stared at him for a moment, then shrugged. 'Makes no matter, if you can thin beets. I should never have planted the cussed things. I've got right next to twelve hundred acres of wheat and thought I'd try a little stand of beets. Big pain in the ass, all this babying and thinning …'

And so they started to thin beets for Bill Flaherty and would have gone in and out and been done and the boy would have gone on with them to California and all the other places except that it rained.

There had been showers now and again that kept them out of the fields for an hour or so because when the soil was wet it stuck to the hoe and they couldn't cut the plants off.

But now it rained, hard, for a full day and it took three more days for the water to dry off the fields, three days of nothing to do but sit and watch the sky and fields and wait. The Mexicans were very good at it, waiting, but the boy hated it after the first day.

It was not that the place was bad. Flaherty was as nice as others had been mean. He went into town and bought a twenty-five-pound bag of pinto beans and ten pounds of hamburger and twenty pounds of flour and gave it all to the Mexicans to cook and eat while they waited. Everybody was well fed and had fat on their lips and one night they had what the old Mexican called a *fandango*, which, the boy learned, was a dance.

They cooked and ate early and cleared away a place in a machine shed for a dancing area and one of the Mexican men had a guitar the boy had not seen before and another used a harmonica and the music mixed with the summer night in some way to make it seem more than just a guitar and harmonica.

Soon many of the Mexicans were dancing, the men one way and the women another way, round in circles, and the old man pulled the boy into the shuffling dance around the centre of the machine shed in the pale light of one bulb hanging from the high ceiling.

At first the boy did not feel the music and simply stepped as they stepped, but then it took him and he was moving his feet to the guitar and harmonica and trying not to stare at the circle of women dancing because they had all started to perspire through their damp white shirts and some of them were not wearing undergarments and it was then, just then, that he saw Lynette.

Bill Flaherty had heard the music from the house and brought his wife, Alice, who was large and round and seemed to be all smiles, and his daughter to watch the Mexicans dance. His daughter was named Lynette and the boy saw her and could not think.

She had long dark hair and an oval face and deep brown eyes and was perhaps seventeen and tall and slender and moved to the music as she stood next to her father and watched the Mexicans dance.

And me, he thought, I am here and she is watching me as well, but he could not tell if she even noticed him. She stayed a few minutes and went back to the house and Bill and Alice followed her a little while later. The next day the ground was dry and they went back to hoeing, and nothing more happened.

Except that the boy could not stop thinking of her, of Lynette, standing in the pale light watching them dance. When they finished the eighty acres and Bill paid them, the Mexicans started to walk down the driveway and the boy followed, his hoe and feed sack over his shoulder. But Bill stopped him.

'Where are you from?' Bill looked off at the beet field.

'I'm with them.'

'Yeah, I know. But you're not a Mexican and I thought ... well, let's try it another way. Can you drive a tractor?'

The boy had driven tractors on his uncle's farm, had ploughed and disced and even drilled seed, but he merely nodded.

'I need help here, for the rest of summer. Someone who can drive a tractor. I've got a bunch of lease land I've got to work up and get ready for winter wheat planting ...'

And here a picture of Lynette entered the boy's mind. He had been thinking of going on with the Mexicans because he was feeling like a man of the road now, with some money in his pocket and another hill to get over – a phrase he'd heard in a country-and-western song – but the clear picture of Lynette came into his mind and he opened his mouth and said, 'What would it pay?'

Bill looked at him and back out across the field and dipped a pinch of snuff into his lower lip. 'Five a day and food including Saturday and Sunday if you want to keep at it.'

'That comes out at thirty-five dollars a week.'

Bill nodded. 'A hundred and fifty a month if you work straight through.'

'I make eleven dollars a day hoeing beets.'

Another nod. '*When* there are beets to hoe. But when it rains or the beets are done, so are you. I'm offering steady work here for the rest of the summer.'

Again Lynette was there – a clear picture. The boy nodded. He'd seen her exactly twice, she was at least a year older than he was and yet he could not stop thinking about her. 'When do I start?'

By this time the Mexicans were at the end of the driveway and he thought to run after them and say goodbye but he stopped, thinking of Lynette, and then they turned the corner onto the road, walking all in white to the next job, and were gone and he did not see them again and would never in his life see them again.

He walked with Bill back into the yard and it was in this way he came to work a steady job and to fall in love for the first time.

FOUR

He never once spoke to Lynette.

Bill set him up in a small trailer next to the machine sheds that had once been used for camping but was now falling apart. It had a bunk across the end covered with mouse droppings and a small table next to the bunk. No lights, no heat, and when it rained it leaked like a sieve.

'You won't be in here that much,' Bill told the boy. 'We work all the time summer and fall. You'll be working from light to dark and then some.'

Except that it wasn't work, not like hoeing beets had been. It was just sitting driving a tractor. Bill had two large Case diesel tractors and it only took him a few minutes that first day to teach the boy how to refuel and run one of them. He hooked the diesel onto a disc and sent the boy off to work the fields he'd leased.

The fields were a good three miles from his farm and once the boy was there working, Bill kept him there until well after dark. Alice drove out in a pickup and brought him cake and sandwiches for forenoon lunch, a full hot meal in lard buckets for midday dinner, cake and sandwiches again for afternoon lunch and then a full supper, always taken in the field so he could keep working.

He had thought at first they might send Lynette with the food but it was always Alice, always good food, more than he could possibly eat but always Alice. She brought him coffee to drink in a Thermos and he hated coffee but drank it anyway, with sugar she brought in an old peanut butter jar, to keep awake on the droning tractor he was driving.

There were no lights on the tractor, for which the boy was grateful. Just at dark – close to nine o'clock – Bill would come in the pickup and take him back to the trailer. The boy would fall asleep on the bunk, mouse turds and all. Before daylight Bill would pound on the side of the trailer to wake him. He would just have time to stop at the outhouse, eat a stand-up breakfast at the tailgate of the truck – a thick-bread sandwich with eggs and bacon between the slices. Then Bill would drive the boy back to the field, dozing all the way, to refuel the tractor and start discing again at first light.

The boy prayed for rain, prayed to get sick, prayed for the tractor to break down, prayed for Bill to get sick, prayed for lightning, prayed for the very earth to swallow the tractor and end the work. But all he got was good weather, the roar of the poorly muffled diesel and the endless, endless North Dakota fields. He thought of many things; he thought of *all* things. Tractor thoughts. He thought of love and making love and what it must be like when it is right and would let his mind go until he thought he would cripple himself with desire and of course he thought of Lynette, though he never saw her. He thought of movie stars and cars he would like to own, a hot rod he would build someday and Hank Williams and he sang, at the top of his lungs, trying to harmonize with and sing louder than the tractor, he sang every country-and-western song he knew and then made some up and at last, in the end, he came down to thoughts of revenge. He thought of getting even with everybody who had ever done a wrong thing to him – his parents, bullies, life, a teacher who'd hit him, an aunt who'd called him a shit-kid when she was drunk – thought of all the ways he could hurt them and make them know, *know* that they had done him the wrong way.

And still there were more fields. He worked a week, then another, then another with no break and each Monday morning Bill handed him seven crisp five-dollar bills to add to the beet money in his pockets. He was rich but even if he'd had time off he didn't want to go to town because he was afraid of being found and sent back.

He lived for sleep and lived to see Alice coming with the pickup to bring him food. He would try to get her to talk but she walked along the edge of the field while he sat and ate, picking bits of grass and small flowers until he was done, then took the dishes and leftover food back, all without speaking more than a word or two but smiling at him and nodding and leaving him.

Jail must be like this, he thought after three weeks – except that it doesn't move and they don't pay you.

When it all fell apart and sent him on the run again as a fugitive it was Bill's fault. Or, as the boy thought of it, of course it had been Lynette's fault for making the picture in his mind that kept him there at Bill's farm and then it was Bill's fault for needing to go to town and not coming back.

The boy did not know anything was wrong. He worked the whole day and when it was time to stop for the night it was not Bill who came to take him back to the farm but Alice.

'Bill had to go to town,' she said to him as they drove to the farm. 'He'll be back later.' But there was something in her voice, some tightness that he had not heard before, and he would have thought more of it except that he hadn't heard her voice enough to know for sure.

None of it mattered. He ate a beef sandwich she brought, so hungry that his jaws ached, and when she stopped in the yard near the yard light he was so exhausted he stumbled to the trailer and fell asleep without undressing.

These nights – he thought of them as tractor nights – he didn't sleep so much as pass out. Nothing moved while he slept. His head jammed into the extra pair of pants he used as a pillow, he didn't dream, he just went down. For this reason it was hard to wake him, and when he at last heard the pounding on the side of the trailer and came out of unconsciousness he couldn't think.

He rolled upright, his eyes still closed and his feet on the floor, and he thought, God, I haven't slept at all and here's Bill already, and he stood and went to the trailer door. It took him four tries, swiping his hand across the lever-type handle before he caught it and opened the door to find not Bill standing there but Alice.

She was wearing a terry-cloth bathrobe and her face looked tight in the moonlight, the skin drawn over her cheekbones in something like a snarl.

'Is it time to go back to work?' he asked.

'No. It's two o'clock in the morning. I need you to go to town and get Bill.'

'Get Bill? What do you mean?'

'I mean he hasn't come home yet, which means he's stinking drunk and you have to go get him. If he tries to drive he'll likely kill himself or some other—'

'But I can't go into town—'

'You take the grain truck and drive into Adams. It ain't but nine miles. He'll be at the tavern – there's only the one beer hall – and you go inside and tell him Alice says to come home now. I'd do it myself but it ain't right for a woman to go into a beer hall and pull at her man. Then you take him out to the grain truck and bring him home and I'll deal with the son of a bitch when.'

The boy just now saw the anger in her eyes and thought of all the reasons he couldn't go into town – it wasn't safe, he was too young to go to a beer hall, he didn't have a licence, he needed sleep, Bill was the boss and he shouldn't go in and drag him home, Bill was bigger than he was and what if he didn't *want* to be dragged home – and none of them came out.

Instead he was quiet and she led him to the 1951 one-ton GMC grain truck and she told him how to start it and turned on the lights and he was heading down the driveway when he realized he had never been to Adams and didn't know how to get there. He stopped and jumped out of the truck – it seemed like ten feet to the ground – and ran back to where Alice was standing.

'Just turn left and go straight when you hit the main road. You can't miss it.'

Under almost any other circumstances he would have liked driving the grain truck. He had driven tractors and sometimes he'd driven the '51 Chevy sedan when his parents were sleeping off a binge. He would sneak out and drive the car round the block in the middle of the night. The grain truck was a good chance to practise shifting and working the clutch. But he was worried too much about what to do when he got to town to enjoy the driving.

Alice had been right about Adams. There were just five buildings, which comprised the main street. A grain elevator, a gas station, a dry-goods store, a farm implement dealer and a tavern called simply Pete's Place; ten or twelve houses were scattered out near an old water tower.

The boy stopped the truck in front of the tavern, the only building with any lights showing. There were three cars there and Bill's pickup all pulled in nose to kerb and he brought the truck in that way – though he was worried about getting reverse right and backing out when it was time to leave – but misjudged the length of the truck's front and drove it up on the sidewalk a bit before he got it stopped.

He hesitated at the door of the tavern. He knew about taverns and knew about drunks and hated them both. He had spent many nights waiting in the car outside taverns while his parents drank – sitting there sometimes for two, three hours before he worked up the courage to go in and try to get them to leave. They never did. All the memories came back now, of the fights and the screaming and the tears, and he shook his head. It's all bullshit, he thought, and pushed open the door.

Pete's looked like all the small-town taverns he had ever seen. Down the right was a rough wooden bar with no barstools and a low-to-the-floor galvanized steel-pipe rail for the drinkers to put their feet on.

On the left side there were three tables with metal chairs scattered around them. At the far end of the bar was a large clock on the wall with its hands frozen at 1.30 and the room was lit by a dim bulb hanging from a single wire in the middle of the ceiling.

There was a bald bartender wearing a filthy white shirt, open at the neck, and at the corner of the bar near the rear, where there was a small opening for the bartender to get through, three men stood playing cards.

'*Damn!*' one of the men yelled, and the boy saw

that it was Bill. 'I can't lose!'

Again the boy waited, thinking, I'm not hired for this – to go to a tavern and watch drunks play cards.

But he stepped forward and moved to where the men stood, wondering as he walked what he would say. The money there took it all out of his mind.

The bartop seemed to be covered with money. Twenties, fifties, hundred-dollar bills were piled in front of each man and Bill's pile was huge. The boy couldn't imagine how much money – thousands of dollars? – was in Bill's rumpled pile.

As the boy came close, Bill said, 'I'll bet one, no, two thousand dollars. You want to see what I've got, you'll have to pony up.' He removed some money from his pile with the exaggerated care of the truly drunk, counting bills slowly and putting them in the pot, and the boy stopped about four feet away and stood silently, watching, mesmerized by the money.

The other two men hesitated briefly, and then silently – they seemed drunker than Bill – put the money from their piles into the pot.

'Cards,' Bill said, and the boy saw he was dealing. 'How many?'

One man took two, the other one, and Bill laughed. 'Shit, I need three.' And he dealt himself three cards.

The boy knew poker, as a small boy had watched it played in bars when his mother was drinking and dragged him with her to chip joints in Chicago. A drunk named Casey had taught him the rules of poker when he was four and the boy had played it later, when he set pins in the bowling alley back home. He and the other pinsetters worked for seven cents a line and lived back in the pits where they drank Pepsi and peed out the back window between lines. One of them had a deck of cards and when it was slow they played poker for pennies and the boy almost never won.

After the draw the man on Bill's left looked at his cards, holding them back against his body and staring down his nose, and smiled. 'Your ass is mine this time,' he said to Bill. 'I'll bet all I have.'

He counted money into the pot – it came to just under four thousand dollars, the man said aloud – and leaned back with the same smug smile on his face.

The other man smiled as well and called the bet and then raised what he had left, another seven thousand dollars. 'If you've got the balls,' he said to Bill, 'if you've got the balls …'

Here the bartender stepped in. He had been leaning back watching the game, his eyes worried. 'You're betting your whole soil allotment money.

This is nuts.'

'This,' Bill said, calling the raise, 'is not nuts, this is poker. What have you suckers got?'

The man on the left had a jack-high straight and reached for the pot but the second man laid his hand down. 'Flush,' he said, 'king high.'

Bill had not even looked at his cards and he held them up now and studied them and smiled and laid them down.

'Four ducks – four little deuces. Jeez, am I hot!'

The boy expelled breath and realized he'd been holding it all this time and Bill started to scoop the money in when the fight started.

'You son of a bitch! You held a pair of deuces and bet two grand?'

'When you're hot, you're—' Bill started, and the man on his left took a drunken roundhouse swing at him and hit him on the side of the temple, knocking Bill away from the bar and on top of the boy.

'Stop this crap!' the bartender yelled, but it was too late. Bill came up like a mad bull and charged into the stomach of the first man, driving him back away from the bar and into the wall. The third man, still standing at the bar, turned now and hit Bill first on the back of the head with his fist and then took another swing at the second man, catching him in the forehead.

Had they been sober any of the blows would have caused severe damage but they were all slow and their punches were flabby. The boy scrambled out of the way and was going to watch until it was over but as the three men pushed and swore and bled and hit at each other they came rolling past the boy. Bill saw him and said through his teeth, 'The money, get the goddamn money!'

The boy nodded and moved to the bar and grabbed the money. There was too much for his pockets, so he tucked his T-shirt in and jammed it down inside past his neck until the front of his shirt bulged with it.

The fight had moved towards the door and the bartender waited until the exact right moment and opened the door and kicked–pushed the men outside.

'I don't care what you do outside,' he said, turning back into the bar, 'but I'm sick of you wrecking my bar.'

The boy ducked through the door after them, holding his arms across his belly to keep the money in, and watched the fight. But moving outside had changed the battle – with space around them they backed off, weaving drunkenly and holding their fists the way they thought fighters should hold their fists, taking ineffective jabs and trying footwork that couldn't be done sober in work boots until finally Bill said, 'Jeez, forget it, I'm going home,' and climbed in his pickup, started the engine, backed out and drove off, leaving the boy.

For a moment the boy stood there, realized that he had all the game money inside his T-shirt, and before they could figure that out he moved to the grain truck, started it and after some gear grinding backed it into the street, turned and followed the taillights of Bill's pickup moving away from town.

Bill stopped about four miles out of town and pulled over and was leaning on the fender of the pickup, vomiting, when the boy caught up with him. The boy stopped the truck, put it in neutral, set the brake and climbed down.

'It goes away when I puke – always has,' Bill said when he stood up. 'You got the money?'

Except for some vomit on his bib overalls and those sunken eyes Bill now looked stone-cold sober. The boy dug the money out of his shirt and handed it to Bill. 'I never saw a game like that – so much money.'

'Last year it was Oleson's turn. It just goes around. How pissed is she?'

'Who? Oh, you mean Alice.'

'Yeah.'

'She's mad. She called you a son of a bitch and said she'd handle you.'

'Ahh – that bad. Well, let's not tell her about the money. It would just confuse the whole thing for her.' Bill was lining up the bills and stacking them on the hood of the pickup and he held out a handful of money to the boy. 'Here – your pay for the evening.'

The boy took the money and glanced at it in the light from the grain truck's headlights. He saw a fifty-dollar bill and many twenties and some tens and thought, Jeez, it must be at least two hundred dollars! He jammed it in his pocket and climbed up into the truck, waited for Bill to start off and followed the pickup back to the farm, shifting loosely, easily, his arm propped on the window of the truck, driving with one hand, singing a Hank Williams song in harmony with the engine, his pockets full of money, and he thought, Hell, there ain't nothing to look back for – thinking it in melody like a country-and-western song, thinking, I've got it now, I've got it by the balls, and he smiled because he thought, that was the way a man would think it, not a boy but a man.

FIVE

The boy had just put his head down on his rolled-up trousers that he used for a pillow, his trousers with the money in the pockets, when he heard pounding on the trailer door and Bill was standing over the bunk with a flashlight.

Sleep was still in his mind and the boy opened his eyes and looked up into the light and said, 'What's wrong?'

'Wrong? Nothing's wrong, it's time to go to work.'

Bill turned and left and the boy started to lie back, so hungry for sleep – it couldn't have been an hour – that his eyes almost slammed shut, but Bill turned and pounded on the trailer again. 'Come on, boy – we got work to do.'

And that time it worked and the boy slid out of the bunk and put his feet on the floor and pulled his trousers on and went out to pee and eat a breakfast sandwich as Bill drove the truck to take him out to the field.

'How much money did I give you last night?' Bill asked while they were pouring diesel into the tractor from five-gallon cans.

'I don't know – I didn't count it yet,' the boy lied. He had counted in the yard light coming through the window of the trailer before he went to sleep. A hundred and forty dollars Bill had given him.

'I don't want it back,' Bill said, reading his thoughts. 'It wasn't a lot, was it? Like a thousand dollars or anything?'

'No. I don't think so.'

'I mean I don't care. I just need to know so I can tell how much I won.'

'A hundred,' the boy said. 'A hundred and forty dollars.'

'Oh. Jeez, I was hoping it was more. I wanted to go over twenty-one thousand – the way it is, I'm shy by seven hundred dollars or so.'

'You won twenty thousand dollars?'

'Almost. But Oleson, he won over twenty last year when we got our soil money from the bank and I just wish I could have won more than he did – you know, just to say it when we're sipping a beer and rub his ugly face in it.'

He left the boy just as the sun edged up and the boy started discing on a field that was a mile long. It was all he could do to stay awake and finally he stood and sang at the top of his lungs to keep from falling asleep. He had decided to hell with it and was going to stop the tractor and sleep when he saw Alice coming with the pickup to bring the forenoon lunch.

He was moving close to the end of the field and she drove round and waited where he would end the round.

She smiled at him and gave him cake and sandwiches and a Thermos of coffee, which he drank first while it was still warm, hoping it would keep him awake.

She did not leave while he ate this time as she always had before, but instead sat in the truck with the door open, while he sat on the ground leaning back against the wheel a few feet away chewing the food and staring out at nothing.

'Was there a woman?'

The question came so suddenly that the boy jumped. He looked at her. 'What?'

'Woman,' she repeated. 'Was there a woman?'

'I don't know what you mean—'

'I mean last night at the bar. I know he played poker. He's always a bad one for cards. And to drink now and then. I can understand that. But I want to know if he had a woman there at the bar with him when you went in for him. Was there a woman?'

He looked out across the field again, chewed and swallowed. It was a meatloaf sandwich and tasted so good he didn't want to swallow but keep chewing. 'No. Just men.'

Alice looked intently at him for a moment, then nodded. 'Good. I've put on weight these last two years and I worry that he'll go to wanting skinny women. I read about it in a magazine, that men want skinny women with big breasts. Is that right? Is that what men want?'

Talking like this made him uncomfortable, made his stomach tighten, and he looked at her out of the corner of his eye and saw that she had been pretty before the weight, and wasn't that fat and was still pretty, and he thought, I have never talked with a woman about breasts before and I am not a man to know what men want, but he remained silent and she kept talking.

'Of course you read all these things and they don't mean Shinola but I did want to know if he had a woman at the bar. Especially if she was a skinny woman …' She let it hang and he realized that he was expected to answer again.

'No. No woman. Just men.' And he had to turn away because she was leaning forward and down from the cab and he could see the swell of her breasts above her dress and there was a little perspiration on them where they came together and he couldn't stop staring at them, at the dampness of them.

'Well, that's all for the good.' She straightened.

'Are you done eating? I'd better get back to the house and start cooking dinner.'

She took the bucket and the Thermos of coffee and drove off and he went back to the tractor and started it and began to disc. He worked all afternoon up to dark when he saw Bill coming for him and if he didn't force his mind to think of other things it stuck on the way Alice's breasts had looked with the faint sheen of sweat on them when she'd leaned down and asked if men liked skinny women with large breasts.

They drove into the yard just as it turned dark and the boy was so tired he'd fallen asleep in the truck. Because he was dozing it took him seconds to realize what Bill said as they turned into the driveway.

'Damn,' Bill mumbled. 'A sheriff's car is here. I'll bet Oleson was pissed about losing that money and wants the law to get it back for him!'

Bill parked and they got out just as a deputy came from the house with Alice.

'He wants to talk to the boy,' Alice said to Bill, and the boy thought, Shit, the Mexicans were right. They have been looking for me.

'I got a report on a runaway and I heard you have a new hired kid out here,' the deputy said. He was tall and had a stomach that hung over his gun belt but his shoulders were wide and he looked strong. And mean, the boy thought – something about him had an edge.

'What's your name, boy?' the deputy asked, and the boy gave him a phoney name.

'You got some paper with your name on it? A licence or something?'

'No.'

'I think you're lying, boy. About the name. You come with me and we'll straighten it out.'

'Hell, Jacobsen, he's a good worker. There ain't nothing wrong with him.' Bill stopped him with a wave. 'He busts his balls for me.'

'Fine. If he ain't the runaway I'll bring him back here. But there's a poster and I've got to tell you he looks close to the picture. Get in the car, boy. The front seat.'

The inside of the squad car smelled like booze and puke and he settled into the seat with his knees near the shotgun bolted in the floor bracket and thought of how it would be to go home. He no longer had a home, in his mind, and if the sheriff had the right picture they would send him back and he didn't think he could stand it.

The deputy drove in silence – breaking it only to make a report on the radio – until they came to a town, the boy fighting sleep all the way so that he missed the sign that said the name of the village.

'We get out here,' the deputy said, parking by a two-storey brick building and pointing to a side door. 'Wait by that door. Don't run.'

'I won't,' the boy said, and for the first time actually thought of it. Maybe he *could* do that, could run.

The deputy locked the car and then came to the door, pushed it open and made the boy go up a set of stairs inside. They were cement steps with steel pipe for handrails, dimly lit by a bulb hanging at the top.

At the head of the stairs there was a steel door and on it was stencilled the word:

JAIL

'Inside,' the deputy said. The boy pushed at the door and then pulled when it didn't open and went into a fifteen-foot-square room with a metal desk and a table with a coffeepot and hot plate on top of it and some filing cabinets along a wall to the right. On the left wall there were three steel-barred cell doors. Two stood open and one was closed with an old man sleeping inside on a metal-frame bed that folded down from the wall and hung on chains.

'Empty your pockets,' the deputy said. 'There, on the table. Everything, and I do mean everything or I'll kick your ass until it's a ring around your neck.'

The boy had a dilemma about the money. He had an old pocketknife he'd picked up somewhere and some change and that was it except for all the money he'd made and what Bill had given him from the poker game, which he had kept with him, stuffed down tight into every pocket. He thought of holding the money back but the deputy sounded like he meant the ass-kicking thing and if he searched the boy and found the money it might go worse for him.

He took the money out and put it on the table.

'What's this?' The deputy had been watching while he drank a cup of coffee from the pot on the hot plate. 'You've got a lot of money there, kid. How much is it?'

The boy said nothing, and stood looking at the money lying in a rumpled pile on the table.

'Come on, boy, save me counting it.'

'I don't know for sure. I earned it hoeing beets and working for Bill. It's all mine.'

'Well, yes, that's one way of looking at it …' He scooped the money up, folded it neatly and put it in his pocket.

'That's my money,' the boy repeated.

'Shut up, kid.' The deputy hit the boy in the shoulder. It was a straight jab and not nearly as hard as it could have been but the boy felt as if he'd been struck with an iron hammer. He slammed sideways into the wall and fell down on one knee and thought, Jesus, I hope he never cuts loose on me.

'Way I see it, your folks want you back and there's no mention of money—'

There was a phone on the desk and it chose that second to ring.

'Damn.' The deputy picked the receiver up and held it to his ear. 'Sheriff's office. Yeah. Yeah. No.' Here his voice changed, softened. 'Well, I can't leave just now, I've got me a fugitive.' He paused, listening. 'How long is he going to be gone?' Another silence, then he took a deep breath. 'I'll be there in ten minutes.' He turned to the boy. 'Get your ass in that middle cell.'

The boy moved from the wall to the cell, hesitated and was pushed through by the deputy. The door slammed shut behind him and the lawman left without speaking.

The jail was quiet except for the rasping breath of the old man in the next cell, and the boy sat on the cot that hung off the wall. He breathed in deeply, then let it out and thought, Shit, he took my money. Maybe if I talk nice he'll give it back to me …

'You get your butt out of here.'

The voice startled him and he jumped and looked across at the old man. He was still on his back, still had his eyes closed and appeared to be sleeping soundly.

'What?'

'Leave. Now. Jacobsen'll be gone an hour at least while he gets sweaty-belly with Beverly Dalton. You can cover a lot of ground in an hour.' The old man still lay with his eyes closed, talking softly. 'Get to the highway and start hitchhiking. Head west. Beverly and her husband, Clyde, live east. You get a ride quick and you'll be sixty miles away before that deputy gets back.'

The boy leaned against the wall. 'Maybe you haven't noticed, but I'm in a cell.'

'Push on the door. It ain't locked.'

The boy stood, pushed and the door swung open easily.

'It's all for show. The locks don't work and they haven't had them fixed – going on two years and more. Now leave, I'm sick of talking.'

'But I'll be a fugitive – a jailbreaker. He'll come after me. I'll go to prison.'

'Like hell you will.'

'Well then, why don't *you* run?'

'Because I am a studier of jails. It's how I live.

You're young and there are other things for you to do ... You're also using up your hour by talking.'

The old man became silent then and the boy walked to the door without quite meaning to and opened it without quite meaning to and walked down the stairs and out the door and broke out of jail without quite meaning to and kept walking until he was at the edge of town and he stuck his thumb out when he saw headlights coming.

The car passed, and the next, and the boy felt that he should be worried but he wasn't. He thought, That big son of a bitch took my money and I'm pissed. And it became a force that made breaking jail and running the right thing to do, a litany that helped him to keep his thumb out, and the next car stopped.

He almost didn't get in. The car was a '49 Plymouth and seemed on the edge of falling apart. That didn't worry him as much as the driver did. He was a small round man with black hair so long it hung over his collar and over his thick glasses that shone so brightly in the light reflected from the dashboard that they seemed to glow in the dark. He did not look weird so much as like a stranger, like he didn't belong anywhere. But it was the only car to stop and the boy felt there wouldn't be another, so he climbed in and settled back into the passenger seat.

The man did not stop talking.

'I am American not yet but I will someday to be citizen. Enclish already I am knowing and nearly enough for testing: if you to ask what President with which date, I know, and how the Congress works, and already I have a fine car and a licence to operate. Is this not a fine car?' Before the boy could say anything he continued. 'In Hungary such a car would not be possible. It is a Plymouth and has a wonderful sufficiency of controls and handles. More than any car I have seen in Hungary. In Hungary such a man to have this car would be a very high official. Here I bought this car with just four months' wages working at the Algonquin Hotel in the city of New York. So many dirty dishes I have never seen. Dishes they have for every little thing and they put dishes on the tables that are not even used. And still they must be washed ...'

After a word or ten or fifteen the boy did not hear them any longer except in groups or if the man said something that caught his interest. '... many fine women', or '... the tanks used machine guns to shoot into windows',

I am now really a fugitive, he thought. He was still exhausted and should have slept but fear kept him awake and his thoughts ran together. I have escaped jail and I am on the run and the son of a bitch took all my money so I can't even eat, hundreds and hundreds of dollars more than I've ever had, more than I'll maybe ever have again. The bastard took it all and they're probably searching for me now and setting up roadblocks or something—

'Portland.'

The boy snapped back. His eyes had started to close and sleep was like a heavy quilt on his thoughts, coming down until the single word struck him. 'What did you say?'

'I am going to Portland. That is in the state of Oregon. Where is it that you are to be?'

'Oh. Sure. Well, I have an uncle in Portland' – the lie came easily – 'and he wants me to come out. I was working on a farm but the work ended so now I'll go visit him for a while. Sure. Portland is fine. I'll go out there and visit my uncle' – Shut up, he said to himself, you're talking too much – 'for a while.'

But the driver didn't think it strange that the boy spoke so long and he merely nodded. 'Company will be good to have.' If he thought it odd that a boy was hitchhiking at night across North Dakota he didn't show it and went back to his incessant stream of words. He spoke now of

New York City and how grey it was and how green the fields in the prairies were and how farmers in Hungary would not believe the farms in America, which he pronounced 'Ammarreeca', and the boy put his head back against the door and let the warm night air blow on his face and closed his eyes and went to sleep and there was not the slightest sign that the next day the man sitting next to him would be dead.

The sun was coming through the back window of the car and cooking the back of his head. The boy had not had a haircut for weeks now and his hair was thick shaggy and the sun heated the hair and seemed to bake his head and it was this which awakened him.

His thoughts came back slowly. He saw the fields going by the car and felt the stiffness in his neck and the heat on his head and saw that he had drooled on his shoulder. He wiped the side of his mouth and remembered at the same time that he was a fugitive and then he turned to see the driver glance at him and smile.

'You are awake. So hard you slept I thought you were dead. I stopped at a place that was open for food and you slept without knowing.' He took a sip of coffee from a paper cup and nodded to a bag between them on the seat. 'There is coffee for you there and some of the round pastries …'

The boy opened the bag and found a paper cup of coffee, which he drank. It was cold and too strong, bitter, but it cleaned his mouth and made him more alert. He looked in the bag again and saw at least a dozen doughnuts, the kind dipped in sugar with the granules sticking to the sides. And he was so hungry, starving, that he ate six of them without thinking, as a dog or wolf would eat, cramming them into his mouth and barely tasting or chewing them.

'An appetite is good,' the driver said. 'But do not make yourself ill—'

And he died.

Later the boy would try to place the sequence of it all in his thinking, the way it happened, and by doing so he hoped to find out in some manner why it would happen. But at the moment, the Hungarian's death came so fast that there was no time to think.

There were pheasants all over North Dakota. Somebody had told the boy that they were imported from China years before, for hunters, and they had increased until it was hard to drive a mile without seeing two or three on the road. In the mornings they came from the brushy fencerows, where they lived, to the shoulders of the roads to gather small pellets of gravel for their gizzards.

Normally when cars roared past the pheasants simply crouched and froze. Now and then they would jump into flight away from the shoulder and sometimes they would jump up and fly in front of the vehicle. Usually, when they hit a car, they rose slowly enough so they hit only the bumper, or grille, though such an impact could cave in a grille or actually dent a fender or smash a headlight.

But if *everything* went wrong they would jump a little early, fly a bit higher and hit in the middle of the windshield.

The Plymouth had a two-piece windshield with a brace down the middle, and a large cock pheasant timed it precisely to leave the ground and strike the windshield in front of the driver's face.

At slower speeds the damage might have been a cracked windshield and a dead bird. But the Hungarian was happy with the car and the morning and sipping coffee while he drove and he had accelerated to nearly eighty miles an hour. At eighty miles an hour a four-pound bird hitting a windshield exerts enormous force. Still, had the bird hit the windshield to the side it might have only broken the glass a bit and bounced off.

But when the pheasant saw the car coming, it turned directly away from the vehicle at the last instant and so was in line with the car when it struck, presenting a much smaller area for impact.

The pheasant blew through the windshield like a cannonball. The car was immediately filled with feathers, and a spray of blood and pheasant guts covered the boy. The shards of glass stripped off the skin and outer surface of the bird but the piece remaining weighed almost three pounds and this chunk of gore, filled with bone, hit the exact centre of the Hungarian's face at effectively eighty miles an hour.

It did not kill him instantly. The force of the bird snapped his head back and broke his neck and cut off all motor responses to his body. His right foot had been directly on the accelerator but he had turned it slightly just before the impact so when his leg jammed down, the foot slid off the pedal and the accelerator popped up and the car began to decelerate.

All this in less than a second.

The boy looked up, saw the feathers and splatter across the windshield, turned to see the bird hit the man's face and felt the car begin to slow. All in a second.

For another second, a little more, the car stayed in the same path. The driver's arms had not moved and did not move for several beats and the car held its course down the highway.

But it was just for a moment. Then the body relaxed, the left hand let go and the right pulled slowly, released, pulled down and steered the car – still doing close to sixty – off the road.

In this part of North Dakota there were no ditches. That was all that saved the boy. The road went to shoulder and then to prairie and the car hit the tall grass, then crossed that into a ploughed field, slamming into the furrows and ruts so hard the boy was thrown against the ceiling.

'Goddamn!'

He was thrown up and down, from side to side amid flying doughnuts, coffee, feathers and pheasant guts and blood as the car slammed through the ploughed furrows in flying dirt and dust to finally, finally come to a stop.

The boy realized he had closed his eyes and he opened them now. The inside of the car was a mess and he wanted more than anything to get out but the driver was leaning back against the door jamb, his face a pulp.

'Goddamn goddamn goddamn…' It was a whisper and he didn't know he was saying it, knew only that he had to do something and didn't know what or how or anything.

He reached across the car and touched the

Hungarian's arm, pushed with his finger, but there was no response and he saw now that the driver wasn't breathing any more and knew that he was dead.

'God—'

The motor was still running and he turned the key off, amazed at how incredibly silent it became. Somewhere nearby he heard a meadowlark call from a fence post, then nothing and he thought, What am I going to do?

Help, he thought. I need to get help. But he didn't know why. The man was clearly, awfully, messily dead – there was nothing to be done for him. And the boy was a wanted man; he thought that way, not as a wanted boy but as a wanted man.

He pulled down on the door handle, opened the door slightly, sick now at the sight and smell of the mess that the inside of the car had become; wanting to puke, he stood out of the car, away from it.

A pattern came into his thinking. Not so much ideas as a pattern of what had to be done. He would have to leave. There was nothing of him in the car and it would help nobody if he was found. He would have to leave and when he came to a place with a phone he could call the police and tell them of the accident and they would come and, well, do whatever they did. That didn't matter.

What mattered, what he saw in the pictures in his mind, was that he had to leave and he slammed the door and moved away from the car and looked back to the road and saw that no cars were coming. He trotted to the side of the road and began walking and for the first time looked down at his clothes. The trousers were all right but the T-shirt was spotted with a little blood.

'Damn!'

Well, nothing for it. He had no other clothes, had nothing. The sheriff's deputy had taken him from Bill's without his clothes. He took the T-shirt off and thought his face must be spattered too. While walking, trotting really, he spat on the shirt and used it to clean his face.

Shirt still off, he had moved along the road for ten minutes, then another five, a good mile west of the wreck, maybe more, when he heard the sound of a car coming, the slick whine of tyres on asphalt. He wondered if he should try to hide but there was nowhere to go – the fields went flat away from the road, nothing higher than a dirt hump for at least a mile, maybe more.

So he kept walking. Whoever it was must not have seen the car off in the field – how could they miss it? – or if they saw it didn't care and he tried to make himself what he wasn't, tried in his mind to be neither part of the wreck nor a fugitive.

The car slowed. He didn't turn but it slowed and came to a stop next to him.

'Going to Clinton?'

The boy turned. An ancient woman wearing a pair of bib overalls and a work shirt sat in the front seat of an old Dodge – the boy guessed a '34 or '35: one of the old black ones. He only knew of them because he'd once watched a boy who had one try to make it into a hot rod.

'Sure,' he said. 'Clinton, sure. How far is it?'

'Upwards of thirty mile,' the woman said. She was round. Not fat but round. 'Too far to walk in a day but I'll give you a ride most of the way there if you like. My name is Hazel.'

'Thank you,' the boy said, and opened the front door and got in, thinking, How can she have gone past the Plymouth sitting out in the field and not seen it? Sitting there with a boy in it and not seen it? But before they'd gone a mile he found out why.

The woman sat, looking straight ahead, a round head in the front seat, and she didn't talk and she didn't look left or look right. She concentrated on her driving, grasping the wheel with an almost frantic grip, both hands, and when she got the car up to thirty miles an hour she stopped accelerating. Thirty it was, thirty it would be as they ground along.

The boy leaned back in the seat – resting his bare back on the upholstered fuzzy cloth, it seemed to be woven with dust built into the fabric – and watched out the side window at the fields crawling by but didn't see anything. His eyes burned in the wind coming through the open window and he thought, I have nothing but crap for luck. I make some money and the law takes it away. I get a ride and ... He thought suddenly of the Hungarian man and how he looked, dead, and felt ashamed for complaining about his luck. If he'd lost the money at least he'd got away from the law and hadn't been sent home. Home? he thought. He had no home. Not any more. He'd never had much of one but now it was all gone – from his thinking and, he hoped, from his memories. His luck wasn't that bad; he'd got away from the law and wasn't hurt in the wreck and he was moving ...

Moving slow, he thought, looking out of the corner of his eye at the lady and at the speedometer seemingly glued on thirty. But moving. It could have been worse.

He closed his eyes for a moment, just a moment – or so it seemed – and when he next opened them the car was stopped and when he looked out he saw he was parked in front of a small farmhouse and the old woman was no longer in the car.

He opened the door and stood away from the car and looked around. It had once been a functioning farm, but years earlier. There was an ancient barn that needed paint and something to prop up the sagging roof. A brick silo with a wooden roof half gone. Some wooden sheds and an outhouse and a small white house that was the only thing in good repair. The farmhouse looked freshly painted and seemed to have an almost new roof and a neatly painted picket fence and a neatly mown rectangle of grass in front. Out back was a garden with clean rows of lettuce and carrots and beans. Everywhere else, out around the house and by the barn and sheds and lying out in the fields around the house, were parked old pieces of farm machinery. Most of it dated back to horse-drawn days: cultivators, swatters, corn and potato planters, seed drills, trip rakes and John Deere mowers. The boy had watched his uncles use horses and knew something of working them and that some farms still used them in the winter when tractors were hard to start, but this equipment was so old the wheels had wooden spokes and iron tyres, so old the wood was rotting.

'You're up.'

The boy turned and saw the old woman coming out of the house carrying a work shirt.

'You seemed tired and I saw the blood on your shirt and figured you for a nosebleeder so I let you sleep. Figured you needed rest. I took your shirt to wash.' She walked while talking and was in front of the boy and handed him the shirt. 'This is one I … had. You take it and cover yourself. I'm cooking some food and I won't feed a person unless he's properly covered.'

She had the strangest way of talking in clipped sentences that never seemed to want an answer. The boy put the shirt on and buttoned it. It was too big by a size but he rolled the sleeves up and tucked it into his trousers and followed her back into the house.

The inside was like a picture he'd once seen in a library book of a fairy village. There seemed to be glass cases or shelves in every corner and they were all filled with knick-knacks; tiny porcelain figurines and animals, little bouquets of porcelain and glass flowers, painted plates, small silver spoons, ironed lace curtains and a crocheted tablecloth on a hardwood dining table in the middle. Off to the back was a kitchen, and a small doorway at the right led to what the boy supposed was a bedroom, but this main room, this sitting–dining room dominated the house. It was like a museum. On one wall there was a large tinted colour photograph of a young man in a pilot's uniform with a flight helmet and raised goggles on his head. Across the picture diagonally there was a narrow black satin ribbon and on the wall next to it was a framed newspaper obituary and a telegram with a black star on it.

'He was my son,' the old woman said, and then disappeared into the kitchen and came out with a bowl of stew and corrected herself.

'*Is* my son – he is Robert and he *is* my son, not was. He was a pilot in the Pacific. Flew one of them P-38s and there was a fight and the Japs shot him down—'

Hazel put the stew down and looked at the picture, her eyes tearing. 'He was something. When it rained of a hot day Robert would take off all his clothes and sit in the yard in a puddle. Just sit there laughing.' Her eyes changed, grew hard. 'I didn't even get the body back. The son-of-a-bitch army kept it and wouldn't give it back to me. They said he was missing. They said they couldn't find him. Bullshit. 'That's all lies,' she spat, her voice a hiss. 'That's lies they tell when they don't want you to know what really happened. He's probably in one of them secret camps. Where they keep them after the war.'

She turned and went back into the kitchen and came back with bread. 'I get magazines with stories in them. I read about them camps – the ones where they keep soldiers so they don't bring diseases back to this country …'

She trailed off and gathered bowls to put on the table and when she had placed them she looked at the boy. 'Hands.'

'Pardon?'

'I want to see your hands, see if they're clean. I won't feed those with dirty hands.'

The boy held his hands up and she took them and turned them over, then back. 'Wash,' she said. 'In the kitchen at the sink you'll find soap and water. Wash them good or you'll take sick.'

He went to the kitchen and it was like stepping back into the past. On the left side there was a big wood cook stove with warming ovens sitting high above the cooktop, all black, trimmed in shiny nickel. Near it, beneath a window looking out on the fields with their old farm equipment, there was a sink with a red hand pump. By the pump was a bar of Lava soap and hanging on the wall next to the window there was a coarse cotton towel. He washed his hands thoroughly and splashed water in his face, dried with the towel and went back into the front room.

Hazel was sitting at the table waiting for him. There were two empty places set on either side of her and he moved to sit to her left but she stopped him.

'Sit here, on my right. That other one is for Robert.'

He nodded and moved round the table to the right and sat and pulled the chair up to the table and it did not seem strange in some way that the other chair and place setting were for Robert. The picture was up there and Robert looked down on them and it seemed the most natural thing in the world to be sitting at the table eating. The food was simple – stew and cold cuts of summer sausage and homemade bread and butter. The boy thought of how the Mexicans had eaten, all taking from the one pot, and of how he had eaten at Bill's, off the tailgate of the truck. He wasn't sure how to eat here, so he waited.

Hazel took a piece of bread and buttered it in a sure rhythm, as she must have buttered it all her life. He waited until she had taken a piece of summer sausage and put it carefully on half of her buttered bread, watched while she slowly cut the bread in half to make a half sandwich, placed the empty half on top of the other half and then put the sandwich in the centre of her plate.

'You make yourself a whole sandwich,' Hazel

said softly. 'You take two pieces of bread, and butter one side of one piece. Then put meat on it and the other piece of bread ...' Her voice was even and carefully enunciated, as if she were talking to a small child. As she spoke she took another piece of bread, buttered half of it, made a half sandwich and put it on the plate beneath the picture.

He did as she told him, working slowly though hunger was tearing at him now. He'd eaten only the half dozen doughnuts before the accident and they hadn't dented the emptiness in him. The bread was cut thick and he rubbed the butter evenly on one piece, took two slices of sausage and made a sandwich. He started to take a bite but saw that Hazel still had her sandwich on her plate and had now clasped her hands in front of the plate. The boy hesitated but did the same.

'Heavenly Father,' she began, paused, took a breath and finished, 'please bless our food and the three of us we pray in Jesus' name amen.'

She ladled stew into the boy's bowl, took up her food and began eating in silence, chewing each bite carefully, looking not quite at the boy, staring past and out the small windows through the lace curtains. Twice Hazel looked up at the picture of the pilot and down at its sandwich with such a look in her eyes that the boy half expected the sandwich on the plate to have a bite taken out of it but when they were done the pilot's plate was untouched.

Hazel took the dishes away, including the one below the picture, and then came back without speaking and went outside.

The boy waited a moment and when she didn't come back in followed her out and they left the yard and went to a small shed, where Hazel rummaged around and came up with a bucket full of tools: wrenches, pliers, screwdrivers, a grease gun, a hammer and some cold chisels.

'Got to work on the swatter,' she said. 'It needs fixing.'

She left the shed and walked across the yard to one of the rows of old farm machinery. At one end stood a large implement with a wooden paddle wheel out to the side, on a platform. On the front of the platform was a sickle bar with teeth for cutting grass or hay or grain and at one end of the platform there was a rack with machinery on it and a metal seat with holes in it that led out to a long wooden tongue with places to hook a team of horses.

'This is a swatter,' Hazel said, putting the bucket of tools on the ground. 'It cuts grain and binds it into shocks. It needs tightening and greasing.'

'I saw one before,' the boy said. 'On my uncle's farm. He said he used to pull it with horses but didn't use it once he got a tractor.' He looked around. 'Do you have horses here?'

'No.'

'Oh.'

'We will, though. Come maybe this fall or next when Robert comes home we'll be getting a team and we need all this equipment ready to go.'

And the boy knew then she was maybe crazy, and he didn't care because it was not the evil kind of crazy like his parents but the soft kind.

'Help me here. Hold this wrench. While I tighten.'

The boy took the handle of the wrench and held it and when the nut was tightened they did another and then another and the old woman showed him how to use the grease gun to grease all the certs on the machine and a rag to wipe the grease off and then on to another machine, a corn planter, and then a mower and then supper with Robert again and then to sleep on the porch and breakfast and working on machines another day, then another, until the boy felt like he belonged to the old farm and the old machines that would never be used.

But he didn't mind. He was a fugitive now, had broken out of jail and was safe here and felt close to Hazel and while there wasn't any money to earn there was food and a place to sleep without worry and it all could have lasted for ever and maybe would have lasted for ever, he thought, except that the county fair came to nearby Clinton.

And so did Ruby.

SIX

There came a morning when they ate breakfast and instead of heading out to work on the machines Hazel brought a clean shirt out of the back bedroom and handed it to the boy.

'Here. We're going to town. You need to be cleaner.'

He hesitated. It had been a week, no, ten days that he had been here with the old woman and Robert and he felt it was not long enough to be safe if they were looking for him. 'I'll stay here and work on the machines.'

'It's the county fair,' she said. Then, turning to the picture, she added, 'Every year the fair comes. We go to it.'

He washed at the kitchen sink and when he came back outside buttoning his shirt she was at the car. She was still wearing bib overalls – had worn them every day since he'd first met her – but they were clean and she had a clean work shirt on beneath the overalls.

'Here,' she said, handing him a folded piece of paper. He looked down and was surprised to see that it was a twenty-dollar bill. 'Man's got to have some money. For spending at the fair.'

'You don't need to give me money …'

'Of course I do. You want it getting out that I don't give my hand money for the fair?'

They drove in complete silence, setting off at thirty miles an hour on the highway for the two miles into Clinton.

The town itself was small – not over a thousand people – and the fair was equally small. It was at the fairgrounds on the edge of town. There was a sideshow banner, a Ferris wheel, a Tilt-a-Whirl, some small car rides for children and a row of game booths. The boy was surprised to see that there were hundreds and hundreds of people there, all scrubbed clean and milling on the short midway. At one end of the fairgrounds there were two large sheds and he could see livestock in the buildings, cages with chickens and rabbits and turkeys, pens with sheep and hogs.

'So many people,' he said to Hazel as they walked from the grassy meadow where the cars were parked. 'Where do they come from?'

'Farms,' she said. 'There's farms all over the place. Town wouldn't even be here except for farmers. 'Sides, it's the last day of the fair and that brings them in a little extra—'

At that precise moment the boy saw the sheriff's

deputy who had arrested him and taken all his money and made him a fugitive. He thought of it that way. He saw not just the deputy – who was walking away from them at an angle across the midway – but the deputy who had arrested him and taken all his money and made him a runner from the law.

He had to hide. If the lawman saw him it would be over. He'd probably go to prison, being a fugitive.

'I have to go,' he said to Hazel, interrupting. 'You know ... to the bathroom.'

He left her walking towards the fair and angled off in the opposite direction taken by the deputy. It led him past the draglines and the Ferris wheel and near the Tilt-a-Whirl.

'Hey, kid you want a job?'

The boy turned and found himself looking at a figure who summed up everything he ever wanted to be in a man. The man wore Levi's so low the crack of his butt showed in the rear and the top edge of pubic hair in the front and a T-shirt with a pack of cigarettes rolled up in the sleeve, one of which he lit now with a Zippo lighter that he snapped open and flicked in an easy motion with one hand. His hair was combed in a perfect greased-back jet-black ducktail and as a final touch of glory he wore heavy-duty black engineer's boots with straps and buckles that looked freshly oiled and polished.

'Doing what?' the boy asked.

The man looked over the boy's head when he spoke, coolly ignoring him, letting his eyes move up and down the fairgrounds.

'I'll give you thirty-five bucks a week to set up and run the Tilt-a-Whirl for the rest of the summer. We're leaving tonight.'

Thirty-five dollars a week from a job with the glory of the carnival seemed unbelievably rich and absolutely perfect for a man who was on the run and the boy at first nodded, then shook his head. 'I can't.'

The man shrugged. 'The world is full of can'ts – it's a word used by losers.'

'No. I mean I *can*. I want the job. But I have some … trouble. I have to stay out of sight.'

'For how long?'

'Just until I leave … you know, for the day.'

The man studied him, looked up and down slowly, looked away again, dragging deeply on the cigarette. 'You're serious.'

'Yes.'

'Is it the law?'

The boy hesitated. 'Yes.'

'You're wanted?'

'I ran off.'

'Oh, hell. We all did that.' He brought his eyes back to the boy, flicked ash neatly off his cigarette. 'Good arms – can you work?'

Can I work? the boy thought – thought of beets and tractor driving and days so bent over he couldn't stand straight. 'Yes. I can work. Hard.'

'Hmmm,' the man said, taking a long drag on the Camel. He thought for a moment more, then shrugged. 'All right. I'm Taylor. You screw me and I'll find you and cut you. Deep.' He fished into his pocket with two fingers and extracted a twenty-dollar bill. 'Here. From your first week's pay. Get your butt into town and get some boots and a T-shirt. You look like a trick. Get back here about midnight to work the breakdown. The law ought to be gone by then – or he'll be so drunk it doesn't matter.'

The boy took the money and started out behind the Tilt-a-Whirl, into some low trees that led off to town, and had gone twenty paces before he remembered Hazel. She would worry. He stopped. It wasn't like leaving the Mexicans, somehow. They had themselves, their families. Hazel had nothing. In the short time he'd been with her she had become something for him; someone inside him.

He trotted back to the midway, stopped in back of the Ferris wheel where the machinery hid him and looked for her. And for the deputy. He saw the deputy first, talking to two women near the draglines. He stood with his back straight and his stomach sucked in and the boy thought, You bastard, you've got my money, you son-of-a-bitch of a thief.

He looked away and at length saw Hazel in her bibs moving towards the livestock barn. He gave one more glance at the deputy, who was still by the draglines with the girls, and moved to intercept Hazel, keeping the sideshow tents between him and the lawman.

'Oh, there you are,' she said as he came up. 'We've got to see the workhorses. There might be some I'd want to buy. For when Robert comes back ...'

'I have to leave,' the boy said because he did not yet know a way to say things smoothly. 'I have to go.'

She stopped and turned and he was surprised to see a tear in the corner of her eye. 'Is it the talk about Robert? Because I just talk, you know. I know he isn't coming back. If I talk about it, it eases the pain of knowing. But if that's it I can—'

'No. I have some other things in my life. Some things I've done. I have to leave,' he repeated. G'damn, he thought, why does it hurt this way? Goddamn! I don't even *know* her. Jeez. 'I'm sorry.

Here.' He dug into his pocket and held out the twenty-dollar bill she'd given him. 'You take this back.'

'No. You go now. Take the money. You'll need it.' She took his hand and with surprising strength folded his fingers back on the bill and pushed the hand back towards his pocket. 'Go. Now.'

And she turned and went into the stock barn, leaving him. He felt some loss he didn't understand, a loss he would always feel and never understand, started after her and stopped, remembered the deputy, his new job, and turned, jogging off towards town, his eyes burning and his feet heavy.

SEVEN

In town he found a dry-goods store and they had engineer's boots – black with black straps and a buckle and thick leather soles. He bought them for seven ninety-five and a pair of Levi's for four dollars and two T-shirts for two dollars each and a set of three pairs of grey work socks.

The jeans he had on were almost falling apart and he went into a back room of the store and changed clothes, ripping the labels off the new Levi's and pulling them down a bit on his hips. He also took off the work shirt and put one of the T-shirts on. In the front again he bought a pack of Old Golds – not cork-tips but straight – and wrapped the package in the sleeve of his T-shirt and rolled the other sleeve up to show his shoulder. He then looked for a Zippo lighter but they didn't have one, so he took a book of matches and bought a nylon unbreakable pocket comb and stuck it in his back pocket.

In front of the store at one corner there was a tap and he wet his hair and combed it back into a ducktail. He was light-haired, almost blond, and his hair did not make a good ducktail but he worked at it and looked in the front window of the store and thought that the Levi's looked too new and his hair to blond but it wasn't bad – much better than he'd looked before – and he liked the way the boots made him taller. He had filled out from all the hard work he'd been doing and felt more like a man now than he had before; felt that he was truly a man on the run from the law taking off with a carnival.

Nearby there was a grocery store. He didn't have a plan except to do as he'd been told and avoid running into that son-of-a-bitch crooked deputy until the carnival packed and left, and he went into the store and bought a box of crackers and three cans of sardines with key openers and two Cokes and two bags of peanuts.

There was a narrow stream running through town, winding behind the stores, and he walked out along the brook a mile and a half, where he found an isolated grassy flat place under some cottonwoods. He sat there with the sound of the running water and ate two cans of sardines and crackers and for dessert had a Coke with a bag of peanuts poured into it and thought it wasn't bad now, had not been bad for some time and in fact the death of the man with the car and the deputy's taking all his money were the only bad things that had happened since he'd run off. He lit a cigarette but only smoked half before throwing it away and then he just lay back on the grass.

He tried to remember his parents, his home, all of it, but he could not picture exactly how his mother looked, though he could recall a little more of his father, their apartment. Instead he remembered the Mexicans and the beets – he could close his eyes and see beet plants still – and the sardines mixed with the crackers and Coke and peanuts made him feel full and he opened his eyes once, closed them, opened them again in a blink and was asleep.

When he awakened it was just into darkness and he would have slept more – the night was warm and soft – except that the end of the sunlight brought out mosquitoes and their buzzing and biting killed sleep.

He had fished and hunted for as long as he could remember and he knew about mosquitoes and how to get rid of them. He made a small fire with bits of dead cottonwood and added green grass and leaves to it to make a smudge. This took away the mosquitoes and he ate the last can of sardines and drank the remaining Coke and peanuts and decided to hell with it, he'd head back for the carnival. It was after ten and by the time he got back it would be eleven. The deputy should be gone and he could help pack the ride or whatever it was he was supposed to do.

There was no moon and it was slow walking in the dim light from the stars. He tripped several times and swore each time and was smudged and dirty when he came back into the lights of town.

The carnival was winding down when he came back to the fairgrounds. Small groups of diehards were still there but the rides were closing and some of the workers were already breaking down. He hung back for a moment, looking for the deputy, and when he didn't see him went to the Tilt-a-Whirl.

Taylor was disconnecting the shaft that ran from the engine to the drive mechanism and glanced up when the boy approached.

'Took your time, didn't you?'

'I didn't want the deputy to see me.'

'He's gone. I paid the bastard off and he left hours ago. Wanted a little tip on the side with Ruby and I told him to blow it out his ass unless he paid. Here, get to work. All those panels need to be loaded on that flatbed. Start unhooking them.'

The boy didn't have the slightest idea what Taylor was talking about – Ruby or whoever and the tip on the side or why Taylor had to pay the deputy off – but it didn't seem like the time to ask questions and he started working at unhooking the floor panels from each other.

He was soon lost in the work. Trying to force the heavy panels apart was nearly impossible and within fifteen minutes he was greasy and his knuckles were bleeding and he was swearing and pissed and wondering if maybe working on a farm wasn't better than this.

'Here, I'll help.'

The boy turned and almost jumped back. He was facing a tall man – he had to be six-five or more – with his head shaved and his eyebrows gone and covered with some kind of black grease that made his face disappear in the darkness except for his eyes and teeth.

'I'm Bobby,' he said, grabbing the side of the panel the boy was hoisting and helping him throw it onto the flatbed truck. 'Taylor's brother.'

The boy nodded and stared at Bobby. He knew it was rude but he couldn't help it.

The man noted the stare and smiled. 'Don't worry. I do the geek show. I just haven't washed the make-up off. Taylor, he likes to get going when the show breaks down. It keeps the farm boys off Ruby. It don't pay after the show is down.'

There it was again: Ruby. He wanted to ask a dozen questions – what was a geek, who was Ruby and why did the farm boys want to be on her and what did Taylor have to do with any of it – but the work was hard, harder than any farmwork, and soon the two of them – Taylor had disappeared as soon as Bobby arrived – were grunting and heaving to get all the parts of the Tilt-a-Whirl on the flatbed. When it was lashed into place Bobby went to the cab of the truck.

'Get in.'

The boy – covered now with grime and sweat and grease, every muscle in his body aching – moved to the off side of the truck and climbed in. Bobby started the engine, reached under the seat, pulled out a pint of Four Roses, took two swallows and handed it to the boy, smiling. 'Want a snort?'

The boy stared at the bottle. It was the same brand his parents drank and he hated the four roses on the label, hated the smell of it, hated the memory of it. But there was Bobby, smiling, the make-up coming off in streaks with the sweat, and the boy was a man now on the run with the carnival so he took the bottle and pretended to sip, handed it back, nearly puking from the taste of it on his tongue.

'Makes the night drive easier,' Bobby said, putting the bottle back under the seat. 'That's all we do – drive all night, work all day.' He delicately worked the clutch and shifted into gear – with much grinding – and started out of the fairgrounds. Other rides were loaded and leaving as well and he had to stop twice to wait for other trucks to get on the highway before he could line it out and shift up into highway speed. The mufflers were bad and the noise was loud but not as deafening as tractors and the boy decided to ask one question. He had many but didn't want to be a bother and thought he would learn things as they came anyway but he was curious about Taylor and wanted to know more about him except that he didn't want to seem nosy.

So he turned to Bobby and asked, 'Where is Taylor?'

It was the right thing to do. Bobby was one of those who just need a start and they keep going and he shifted, grabbed a towel off the seat and wiped some make-up off his face and laughed.

'He's driving the pickup that tows the Ruby wagon. You won't see them until we're all set up in Harken in a couple of days. Taylor, he'll sometimes help break down but he hates to set up. I remember once in – I think it was Hastings – he didn't come out at all until it was time to get the money boxes. Then there was the time in Cordovia when he went home with two farm sisters and I didn't see him till nine days and two towns later …'

The boy nodded and tried to pay attention but it all just made more questions come and the night air blowing in the window was soft and warm and in spite of sleeping all day he was hard tired, bone tired. He closed his eyes.

He dreamed while he slept. There was his mother and she was sitting at a table and she pointed her finger at the window and he turned to see what she was pointing to but he never saw, couldn't see and then he woke up.

It was daylight. Bobby was still driving and the boy closed his eyes again, wanting to see what his mother had been pointing to, but he could not. The drone of the truck worked up through the metal of the doorframe into his skull where he rested his head and he moved away from it, sat up, wiped his mouth.

'Want another snort?' Bobby again held out the bottle, which was now nearly empty, and he shook his head.

'No. It's too early for me.' He'd heard men say that as an excuse to not drink. Never his parents. It was never too early for them. But other people, other men.

'I'll bet you're hungry.'

The boy nodded and realized that he was – starving.

'You'll find some prunes in a bag under the seat. Hand them up.'

'Prunes?'

'Damn right. Good food, keeps you regular – just don't swallow the pits.'

The boy fished under the seat and found the prunes, handed them over. 'I'll wait until later.'

'Later. Shit, kid, there ain't no later. We don't get to Harken until tonight. You'll starve by then. You'd better eat some.'

Another thing that men do, the boy thought – eat like this, on the run. He remembered the meals with Robert, the food on the tailgate at the farm, the pots of food with the Mexicans. Prunes. Jeez. Prunes. He sighed and took a handful and popped one in his mouth, chewing.

'See – they ain't bad. I started eating them with whiskey to take the taste of chicken heads out of my mouth but now I like them. Prunes and whiskey.' He laughed. 'Gives you the runs, but you don't care …'

'Chicken heads?' The boy couldn't help it. 'You put chicken heads in your mouth?'

Bobby looked at him. 'You don't know what a geek is?'

The boy shook his head. 'I don't know anything about carnivals.'

Bobby laughed. 'Not many do. Once you've

been a carny you never look at people the same way again. It's just like being a cop. You know everybody is a loser.'

Not everybody, the boy thought. For sure the deputy, and his parents, but not Hazel and the Mexicans and Bill – but he didn't say anything.

'A geek is a wild man from Borneo who lives in a cage. He's so wild he can't be out with other people and once a day the carnival people throw a live chicken into the cage and the geek bites the head off.'

'You're the geek?'

Bobby nodded.

'Are you from Borneo?'

Bobby stared at the boy, smiled and then shook his head. 'You don't get it, do you? I'm from Michigan. There *are* no real wild men from Borneo. It's a setup. A lie. It's all a bunch of bull to take money from the farmers.'

'Oh.'

'I use make-up and turn my skin black and wear some rags to hide my privates – only let it show a little now and then to get the women to peeking – and sit in a cage pretending to pick bugs off my skin. The suckers pay fifty cents each to get in the tent and see me and then another fifty cents to watch me being fed.'

'You actually bite the head off a chicken?'

Bobby laughed. 'I've bit worse than that, boy. I was in jail in Mexico once and ate a rat. Raw. And I was damn glad to have that.'

Maybe that's why prunes aren't so bad for him, the boy thought. If he has to eat chicken heads and rats.

'If you do it right you can get them to puke. Best night I ever had was seventeen people and nine of them puked. Course it wasn't all me. When I bit the head and I spit blood and shook the chicken around some to splatter blood on the hicks two women started puking. Then another one smelled that and I think it caused the rest to let go. It was great. I left the upchuck on the ground in front of the cage and the smell of it got the next batch going – hey, I had all of Lincoln puking before it was over.'

The boy felt queasy and looked out the window, let the wind blow on his face until the feeling passed. He turned back. A different question – to get Bobby off puke. 'Who is Ruby?'

Bobby stopped talking for a moment, looking out the windshield. 'She's Taylor's ... wife. She dances the kootch.'

'Kootch?'

'Hootchy-kootchy. She takes her clothes off for the farm boys.'

'And Taylor doesn't *care*?'

'You are *so* green!' Bobby snorted. 'Taylor doesn't care what she does as long as she makes money for him.'

Bobby stopped talking then. He finished the rest of the whiskey in one swallow and threw the bottle out on the highway, fished under the seat and pulled out another pint. The boy was to find that while he never saw Bobby actually act drunk he was never without a pint of Four Roses.

'All right.' Bobby slowed the truck and pulled over to the side of the road near some brush. 'The prunes have hit. I have *got* to take a dump.'

He jerked the hand brake on, slammed the door open and was squatting in the brush before the boy had his own door unlatched.

The boy found another bush and peed, listening to the meadowlarks, looking across the prairie until he was done. As he walked back to the truck a car roared by and the boy was surprised to see the driver — he looked like a salesman — give him the finger. He climbed back into the cab and waited for Bobby, who was done in a short time.

'That guy gave me the finger. I don't even know the guy and he flipped me the bird!'

Bobby laughed. 'That's because you're in a carny truck. He saw the ride on the back. Nobody likes carnies.'

Bobby started the truck moving and worked

through the whining of the gears until they were at highway speed again. He was silent while shifting but started talking when they got up to speed. The boy tried to listen – something about a man who would swallow anything as part of a geek act – but he was still drowsy and the sun was high enough to warm his cheek and he closed his eyes and was sleeping again.

EIGHT

In the first week with the carnival the boy learned more than he had in his whole life before that, and in some ways more than he would learn in all the time he lived afterwards. He learned carny rules, carny thoughts, carny lives.

He learned that everybody who wasn't with the carnival and some who were with the carnival were suckers. Bobby taught him that. Along with how to know how much money a man was carrying by the way he stood when he thought he was going to have to spend it, and whether or not a woman would put out. That was how Bobby said it – put out.

'See that one?' he said as they were setting up the ride and two young women were walking by, heading for the stock barns. 'The one on the left? She'll put out. The other one won't but that one will. She'll put out like a machine.'

'Put out what?' The boy had honestly never heard the phrase and while it was true that he thought almost literally of nothing but sex by this time – the condition had worsened as he stopped worrying about the law and being a fugitive and felt more secure – he did not put it together with what Bobby was saying.

'Poon,' Bobby said. 'Poontang, pussy – you know. Screwing. She'll do it, the other won't.'

So the boy looked at the two women. They were both wearing tight jeans and light sweaters and both walked with their hips moving in the way the boy had come to have difficulty watching. He could see no difference between them, no indication of what Bobby meant. 'How can you tell?'

Bobby stared at the women until they were out of sight. 'You get to where you can. It's experience. You just know.'

'I couldn't tell at all.'

'I could. That's all that counts.'

For you, maybe, the boy thought, but he said no more and even later when he saw that it wasn't so and that Bobby didn't really know how to tell and that he never did anything with *any* women it didn't matter. It was still something the boy learned and besides there were other things that Bobby had to teach him.

That all people wanted to lose. Bobby taught him that as well.

'They say they want to win, they say they want to be right, but it's just a bunch of hooey. All they want to do is bitch, and getting shafted gives them something to bitch about. Watch them on the rip games—'

'Rip games?'

'The nickel toss, ring a looie, the sucker ball. They keep coming back even when they know they can't win. They keep trying when it's a dead toss just so they can bitch about it later. They walk away shaking their heads and whining but they always come back. Suckers.'

And while the boy knew that what Bobby said wasn't always true and that all people weren't suckers he thought of Hazel and of the man who died when the pheasant hit him — he came to see what Bobby meant as he worked at the carnival and became more a carny and less a boy.

And it did not take long. By the end of the first day of full work he had learned much and in a week he was pretty sure he knew it all.

When they arrived in Harken Bobby drove out to the fairgrounds, stopped the truck, got out and looked at the area set aside for the rides and smiled up at the boy. 'Same as last year – let's get to work.'

The boy jumped down and they started to unload the panels from the truck. The boy looked for Taylor's pickup but soon they were working so hard he didn't have time to look. They horsed the panels around, locked them together, rigged the seats and locked them in, the two of them working all afternoon and into the evening and when there was nothing left to do Bobby punched him in the shoulder. 'You hungry?'

The boy stood, weaving. He was past tired. Covered with grime that made him look dark, old, creased around his eyes. And he was beyond hunger as well. Nothing to eat all day except for a handful of prunes, and nothing much the day before except peanuts and Coke and sardines and crackers. He was afraid to move, to try walking, sure that he would fall over. 'Eat? Food?'

'Hell, yes – did you think you could live on prunes for ever? Let's hit the gedunk stand.'

Other rides had come to set up while they'd worked – although the boy hadn't had time to stop and look at them – rides and booths, and off to the side was a food trailer with the panels up on the sides showing pictures of hot dogs and hamburgers and Cokes painted in faded colours.

The boy followed Bobby to the stand and stood, dazed with exhaustion, while Bobby talked to the man working the stand.

'You got money?' Bobby turned.

The boy dug into his pocket and pulled out some bills, handed them to Bobby without looking, staring ahead, and within two minutes he was handed two greasy hamburgers dripping with ketchup and mustard.

'Eat 'em quick,' Bobby said. 'Before they spoil on you.'

It was a joke but the boy didn't hear it. He ate the burger in his left hand in three enormous bites, took the one in his right in four – not tasting them – and stood, his hands greasy, not moving, waiting. It was dark and he thought he was supposed to do something, be somewhere, but he couldn't think.

'Go to the truck,' Bobby said. 'Crawl up on the seat and sleep. The carnival doesn't start until tomorrow.'

The boy turned and walked zombie-like to the truck parked at the back of the ride as he was told, climbed up into the cab to lie down and was asleep before his head hit the seat.

The boy slept hard – in a kind of unconsciousness – and did not awaken until the late-morning sun and a roaring prune-and-greasy-burger-induced need to take a dump drove him out of the truck and into the concrete bathrooms by the stock barns at a dead run. He barely made it and came out of the bathroom to see a different world than he'd seen when he'd gone to sleep the night before.

The barn was full of livestock, there were many more booths laid out in a row to make a street between them, and more rides were set up. He was amazed that he had slept through it all, amazed and suddenly very hungry.

The same food trailer was more established now, with a tarp set up over two long tables and folding metal chairs to make a place to sit and eat. The boy went up to the counter and studied the painted menu, fingering the money in his pocket. 'What do you have for breakfast?'

The man in the booth turned and the boy saw that he had no fingers on either hand. 'I have hamburgers or hot dogs. All the time. Which do you want?'

'A hamburger.' The boy tried not to stare at the man's hands. Using his thumbs against his palms like pincers, the man held the spatula and slid the burned-cooked meat onto a bun he'd had cooking on the grease on the back of the grill. He wrapped the burger in a piece of waxed paper. 'Fifty cents.'

The boy paid and turned away to eat. At fifty cents a small burger, he thought, I'll be broke by tomorrow unless Taylor gives me more money. He ate the burger in four bites, bought another, ate it and walked over to the Tilt-a-Whirl where Bobby was starting up the drive motor and doing a test run.

'You work the clutch to make the seats spin hard,' he said over the sound of the engine as the boy walked up. 'There won't be much for the rides to do until dark. But you practise now, and after a bit you know how to work the clutch and can make certain seats spin more than others.'

'Why bother?'

'You look for men with loose trousers and spin them hard. The change will come back out of their pockets and fall into the crack in the seat. Sometimes you'll get a wallet, but mostly change. Taylor, he'll split it with you if he's in a good mood.'

'Split what?'

Taylor chose this moment to arrive. He looked clean, his hair well combed, a cigarette hanging from his mouth.

'I was telling the kid how to work the clutch to get change.'

Taylor looked at the boy. One look, quick, up and down. 'You look better. Dirty, but better. Got rid of that goddamn farmer look.' He inhaled, exhaled, without taking the cigarette from his mouth. 'You help Bobby set up the geek show and shill for him. I'll run the ride tonight.'

The boy did not fully understand what Taylor meant but he didn't ask questions because he didn't want to appear stupid and, in any event, in moments he was busy helping Bobby set up the geek tent – little more than four tarp walls with a zigzag entrance and no roof. In front they put up a wooden platform eight feet square and three feet off the ground. Inside was a small cage set on a wooden platform also three feet high, the cage not over four feet on a side with a thin mesh over the top, held on with pieces of wire, the sides bolted together. As the boy finished tying the tarp off to stakes they hand-pounded into the ground, Bobby hooked up a grubby-looking public-address speaker and microphone and set them all on a raised wooden platform they dragged from the truck. He also had a rubber dog turd, which he put in the cage, and some yellow liquid in a jar he poured on the floor. 'Kool-Aid – but they think it's piss. They think I crap and pee in the cage.' He disappeared again for a few minutes and came back holding a live chicken.

'From the stock barn,' he said. 'They sell 'em for fifty cents.'

He put the chicken in the cage and went off again, came back in a long coat, carrying a can of some dark paste. 'Here, help me make up. Just wipe it on and smear it around – the greasier looking the better.' He took off the coat and the boy saw he was wearing only an old tattered pair of briefs, ragged and stained by make-up and revealing. The boy wiped the grease onto Bobby's back, gingerly at first and then harder until the man was completely dark. In the meantime Bobby had been doing the front of his body and his face, looking in a small mirror now and then to touch up. It was hot inside the open tarp cubicle and his sweat shone through the make-up.

'Go tell Taylor it's time to start barking,' he said, working on his legs and feet. 'Quick, before all this crap runs off me.'

The boy ran to the Tilt-a-Whirl – which wasn't in operation yet – and found Taylor smoking a cigarette and looking at some women walking past. They were older women, not wearing tight clothing and not wiggling like some of the young ones did, but it didn't seem to matter to Taylor.

'Bobby says it's time to start barking, whatever that is …'

Taylor took a drag on his cigarette and flicked it away in an arc. 'It means getting the farmers in. Yeah, I'll start calling. You go out in a kind of circle, over that way to the left, and when I start talking fast you sort of stop and then hurry over and stand in front of the geek tent. Got that?'

'Is that shilling?'

'Just do it. Then when I give you a sign, you go off in a different direction, over to the right, and come to the geek tent again. They'll follow you like the dumb little sheep they are.'

The boy moved off. He hadn't gone thirty paces

when there was a squawk and a hiss and Taylor's voice boomed over the fairgrounds.

'Wild man from Borneo! Untamed and naked and savage! Four men killed capturing him just so you can see him for one thin half-dollar! Come now and watch him feed on live flesh! It's all happening now, right now, on the midway!'

The fair wasn't packed yet – as the boy would find it the next day when all the rides were going and the weekend had truly started – but there were groups of people here and there and the sudden booming public-address system stopped them and caught their interest.

The boy went to a spot where ten or fifteen people seemed to be gathered and trotted through the middle of them, heading for the geek show.

And they followed him. Just like Taylor had said. Followed him until he was standing in front of Taylor, who was up on the platform. The boy stood for a moment, mesmerized. Taylor had taken command of all of them, held them with his voice, his look.

'There, inside that tent, is a man who has never seen civilization. He's as wild as a wolf …'

He looked right at the boy and made a motion with his chin and the boy understood, moved back through the crowd and found another group of people and led them back.

Soon there were thirty of them, all standing watching Taylor.

'Just a half-dollar to see him, one thin half-dollar, two tiny quarters in the box to see a sight never seen by civilized man before!'

He worked them, stroked them, and when they were right on the edge the boy caught it, understood without being told what he should do next and moved forward and put a half-dollar in the cigar box on the platform and went into the enclosure. His timing was perfect and he heard change hitting the box behind him.

When the crowd was in the tent – over twenty of them jammed in the tiny enclosure – Bobby started slamming around in the mesh cage, shaking it so the people would jump back and the women gasp. It was more education for the boy watching Bobby work. He had worked up an act that made the boy think of a minstrel show he'd once seen mixed with the movie gorilla King Kong trying to escape from captivity. Bobby leaped from one end of the cage to the other, nude except for the tattered pair of briefs, his shaved head glistening with the black make-up.

'Arrgh!'

He lunged at the mesh, startling the crowd and even the boy, who was not ready for it and jumped away from the cage. One older woman had to leave the tent. A younger man, probably her son, went with her but came back in a moment.

The boy was not sure how Bobby decided the time was right – he said later it was when the 'farmers are wet-lipped and whip-ready' – but until now he had ignored the other occupant of the cage.

The chicken.

All this time in the small cage there had been the victim chicken. Everybody saw it, everybody knew why it was there, knew that the wild man from Borneo was going to do something with the chicken, something awful, and now, glaring at the crowd, the wild man's white eyes flashing out from the dark make-up, he suddenly jumped and snatched the chicken, which squawked and flapped its wings.

Still he did not hurt it.

'Timing is everything when it's farmers,' he told the boy later. 'You have to time everything perfectly.'

Taylor came into the tent then, with the cigar box. 'It's time to feed now. Many of you know how expensive it can be to keep a wild animal. Please put something in the box to help us support this scientific discovery …'

His voice was soft now, not barking but soft, and the boy was amazed to see people put more money in the box, change and some bills.

Even though they paid, the boy could see they still did not believe it – not all of it. Did not believe in Bobby, did not believe he really was a geek – a wild man from Borneo – and most certainly did not believe he would do anything to the chicken.

They paid their money to get in, and they jumped back when Bobby jumped at them and they were disgusted by the turd in the cage and the puddles of yellow pee in the corners and some of them – young women – kept peeking at his shorts and what they almost concealed and everyone was clearly horrified and sickened by the *thought* of Bobby doing something to the chicken but they did not truly believe he was real or that he would do it.

'Ah, it's all fake,' a young man who had taken his mother outside said, squaring his shoulders. 'I'd get in that cage and kick his butt if they'd let me.'

'It's all bull.' Another young man. Some young women were there, and one of them looked at the second young man and smiled a tight little grin but said nothing. Her face was pale.

And then Bobby did it. With perfect timing he put the chicken's head up to his lips, took it in his mouth and with a tearing motion bit off the head. 'There's cords in 'em ,' he told the boy later. 'In the neck, stringy cords. You got to rip kind of sideways.'

The chicken flapped and spewed blood from the stump of its neck and Bobby made sure the blood sprayed on the crowd, swinging the carcass around and growling until all the people were gone.

'Never more than one chicken per day,' he said, standing out of the cage and spitting. 'It softens the act too much, you start killing chickens all the time.'

The boy helped wipe some make-up off and then went to the food booth while Bobby went off in the coat. The boy wasn't hungry so much as he had a taste in his mouth – he thought he could taste the chicken head and could not stop thinking of what it would be like, the beak, the eyes with the lids opening and closing inside his mouth. Even if you bit quick, he thought, you were going to feel some of that, know that the beak and eyes were there, and he wanted a Coke in his mouth to get out the taste left by thinking of the beak and eyes on his tongue and it was then that he first met Ruby.

He had just taken a Coke from the man with no fingers and was going to head back for the Tilt-a-Whirl when Ruby walked up beside him.

In some way because she was real she was the

most beautiful thing the boy had ever seen.

This was before he had seen much television, so the boy's knowledge of beauty was limited largely to women with enormous breasts he had seen in films – Marilyn Monroe, Jayne Mansfield, Jane Russell were popular in those days and at first glance Ruby very definitely qualified.

She had long blonde hair and was wearing a T-shirt that revealed her 'full-figured bust development', as they put it in the lingerie sections of the mail-order catalogues that the boy and several million other boys frequently read alone, and long legs below an impossibly tight pair of short-shorts.

Her eyes swept over the boy as if he didn't exist. She had been sleeping – her eyes showed it and her tousled hair – and she clearly did not know that the boy knew Taylor or that he worked for him, just as the boy did not know who she was; he just knew she was beautiful, blonde and glamorous and he froze with the Coke halfway to his mouth and stared at her.

As befitting royalty she continued to ignore the boy.

'Give me some coffee,' she said to the man behind the counter. 'I can't get my damn eyes open.'

She swore professionally, cleanly, the way a

gunfighter draws and shoots, and the boy loved her from that instant. Her looks made her alluring, her swearing made her worldly, he was gone. He would have killed for her.

She took the paper cup and drank half the steaming coffee as if it had been iced. She paused to take a breath, drank the rest of the coffee, threw the cup in a barrel near the counter and walked past the boy, artfully brushing her breast against his arm on the way by.

'Close your mouth,' she said without looking at him. 'You'll step on your friggin' tongue.'

He slammed his mouth shut and watched her walk away on her shower clogs, her hips rolling easily, and the man behind the food counter laughed.

'That's Ruby,' he said. 'She goes with Taylor.'

'Oh.' He watched her walk past the Tilt-a-Whirl where Taylor was working and turn off to the right where he could see some small aluminium camper trailers parked. Watched her walk the whole way. Watched her hips and legs and the short-shorts the entire way. 'Oh …'

NINE

The boy learned to use the Tilt-a-Whirl's clutch to whip the cars round, which emptied change from the pockets of the farmers. The best day he had he stripped almost eleven dollars. Taylor was fair and let him keep half of what he stripped and he paid the boy every Friday so the boy always had money to spend on endless hamburgers and Cokes. Never money to save. Never money to own as he'd owned it before the deputy took it away from him. But plenty to spend on his new life. His carny life.

The boy had become a carbon copy of Taylor. He wore his dirty Levi's low, with no underwear, and with a white T-shirt tucked in and sleeves rolled up to hold a packet of Camels without filters, which he could flick-light with a Zippo lighter, and his hair slicked back with Brylcreem to make an almost-controlled ducktail. And he had the look. The hard carny look that said everyone was a sucker or a farmer or both, said everybody was merely something to scorn. Even though the boy did not truly believe it he still had the look.

He had learned much in a short time. How to watch women so he seemed to know something about them, though he didn't. How to talk of them in an appraising way though he was no more knowledgeable than Bobby, who knew nothing and spoke so well he seemed an expert. The boy had learned so much and become so confident that he had become almost completely ignorant and had ceased to know new things and he might have gone on learning more and more and becoming more and more ignorant for ever.

Except for Ruby.

He'd been with the carnival a month before he saw her naked.

They had moved three times, a different town in North Dakota every weekend, and when they moved Taylor and Bobby worked the boy nearly to death. They had to break down the ride, Bobby's geek tent and setup, which doubled later as Ruby's kootch tent and dance platform. All this was loaded on the flatbed truck – and done at virtually a dead run because there was never enough time between shows – and they would drive like hell to get to the new town. Grafton, Hamilton, Minot – a blur of farmers in new overalls and white shirts and women in crisp new cotton dresses.

Taylor and Ruby always rode together in a pickup pulling the camper trailer and Bobby and the boy rode in the flatbed. Since Bobby spent all his time talking and drinking Four Roses from the endless supply beneath the seat the boy only rested now and then and the upshot of all this frantic work and travel was that he never really got to watch Ruby.

She didn't help with work but would stay in her little trailer until they were packed and ready to leave. Then she would get in Taylor's truck cab. When they were set up and working the boy would look over at her on the stand in front of her tent before she drew the farmers inside, trying to get a glimpse. But she was always dressed in the short-shorts and T-shirt – although when parading on the platform she replaced her shower clogs with high-heeled pumps.

'The shoes gets her buns up nice, don't they?' Bobby once said to the boy, who thought it was wrong to speak of her that way because he loved her.

Then there came a night when she had trouble getting a crowd. It was in a town in South Dakota and they had been there four nights. Usually when Ruby started parading and Bobby barked for her – he cranked up what he called 'the hootchy-kootchy rhythms' – men and especially boys would stop whatever they had been doing and gather to watch. But this was the fourth night and everybody who was going to watch her already had. Only two men – both old – had stopped.

Taylor and the boy were by the Tilt-a–Whirl and he pushed at the boy's shoulder.

'Get your butt over there and shill for her,' he said. 'We ain't made beans in this town.'

He often shilled for Bobby on the geek setup but he didn't think Taylor wanted him to see Ruby.

'You mean just outside?' he asked, holding his breath. 'Or on the inside too?'

'Whatever it takes to get the sons of bitches to spend money – move.'

So the boy went to the front of Ruby's stage and looked up at her and Ruby looked down at him and Bobby started the scratchy phonograph with the whiny belly-dance music.

Later, when he was a man, and old, it was hard for him to look back and remember how pretty or not pretty Ruby really was. By then there had been others, and a life, in between. But he knew on that night, that first night, on that night it was not possible for Ruby to be anything but beautiful.

The music whined and scratched and Bobby pitched:

'She comes from the Orient where she was the queen of a sultan's harem — she knows all the secrets of love …'

And the boy went out into the carnival grounds and found men in small groups and led them back the way he did when he shilled for the geek show, though he did not want to leave, even for a moment. Because he *believed* Bobby.

The boy watched her move back and forth on the stage, her pumps clicking in time to the music, her tight short-shorts barely containing the ripple of her, her breasts straining against the thin T-shirt as he had read about breasts straining in every Mickey Spillane book, read and reread until phrases like that were memorized from the worn pages handed from boy to boy, back when he had a home.

She was, simply, everything.

Not just everything about sex or love or lust or carnal knowledge or throbbing or straining or penetrating or moistness or any of the other intense, unbelievably focused thoughts that dominated his life.

She was everything.

Then, on that soft summer night while the

boy stood and looked up at her moving to the scratchy kootch phonograph music coming from the crude PA, she was just everything.

There was not another thing then in the boy's life. Not one. All thoughts, all hopes and desires and dreams and prayers, were for Ruby; life was for Ruby, death for Ruby, his heart, his soul, for Ruby.

And she smiled at him.

Not just a carny smile – or he did not see it as such – not a smile over him or around him or through him but she looked into his eyes and smiled.

'You're going to rip your pants, kid,' she said, and he looked down to where she pointed and was mortified to see the bulge.

'I'm s-s-sorry,' he stammered, but she ground and bumped her hips and laughed softly.

'It's no big thing – and I *do* mean it.'

No more men had arrived by this time, and since it was apparent that nobody else was going to stop, Ruby shrugged her shoulders and breasts and turned off the platform and wriggled back through the canvas curtain to begin the process of fleecing the men of their money.

The procedure was lengthy and complicated. The boy had never seen it but had heard Bobby talking about it with other carnies, bragging about Ruby because he said she was the best he'd ever seen.

'She hooks them like trout,' Bobby said. 'Shows a little of this and a little of that and the poor bastards are broke before they know it – she pu-u-ulls the money out of them.'

It was a matter of finesse.

Men had already paid Bobby to go into the tent itself – a dollar each. With the promise, the hot promise, the hot-night-carnival promise they would see more, would see all. The boy had followed them in.

And inside the tent the world changed. Once in, once that far into Ruby's world, they were gone.

Bobby played the scratchy music and Ruby took things off but slowly, so slowly, pulling the T-shirt up an inch at a time, one ... inch ... at ... a ... time ... until suddenly there they were.

Her breasts.

But not really. Not really and truly because she wore a gauze kind of bra beneath the blouse and you couldn't quite see anything. It was like looking through smoke, though by this time it didn't matter to the boy.

But if they wanted more, if they wanted to see the breasts, there was only one way to do it.

More money.

Bobby circulated with an old felt hat.

'Come on – the girl's got to live. Another half a rock to see 'em.'

And he would plead and cajole, his voice a song, a siren. A fifty-cent piece here, a quarter there, bits of money to see bits of Ruby until finally, almost finally, she stood naked.

Except …

Except for a G-string, a small piece of cloth over her pubic area.

Which, of course, the boy thought of as 'it'. 'It' was right there and he wanted to see all of her but he felt wrong staring and would look away and back, down and back at 'it', and back …

Right … *there*.

Under the little cloth.

There 'it' was …

For more money.

They could see 'it' for just another dollar each. Everybody paid.

Of course the boy didn't have to pay except that by this time he was so caught up in what Ruby was doing that he actually reached into his jeans pocket and pulled out a dollar and handed it to Bobby. Bobby looked at him like he was crazy but took the dollar and smiled and said, 'Sure, kid – your money works.'

The boy had a quick thought, a flash of

wonder at Bobby – how could he do this, work with her every day, see her naked every day, watch her and hear her and smell her? How could he do that and not go insane?

But it passed quickly.

Bobby started the needle on the scratchy record again. Ruby started moving and the boy was transported.

Bobby, the other men in the tent, the canvas walls, the pitiful music – everything was gone once more.

Only Ruby.

Only 'it'.

She danced four or five little steps, did some small gyrations and hooked a thumb in her G-string and pulled it down her leg.

An inch, another inch, until the hair showed, a corner of hair curly and damp-looking in the pale light from the single bulb hanging from the top of the tent.

Another inch, then a snap and the G-string was gone.

'It' was there.

All of 'it'.

The boy didn't know how long he went without breathing. Half a minute, a lifetime; perhaps he'd never breathe the same, quite the same again, for ever.

'All right, boys, that's it.' Bobby's hoarse voice cut in. 'The show's over.'

Grumbling, the old men snorted and swore and rubbed themselves but Bobby was strict and, when they left, he followed them out of the tent.

The boy was transfixed. Frozen. Ruby stood there for a moment, totally nude, facing him – or rather, with her up on the small platform, 'it' faced him. She was totally unself-conscious, relaxed. She took a cigarette from a stool at the back of the stage, lit it, stared at the boy.

He realized he was staring at her, holding his breath, and he exhaled, inhaled, shook all over and forced himself to turn and leave.

'Wait a minute.'

Her voice was flat but lifted at the end – not in question so much as speculation.

'How old are you, kid?'

He had turned away and he looked back.

'Eighteen.' He lied easily but she snorted and blew smoke out of her nose.

'More likely sixteen, if that.'

She paused again, eyeing the boy slowly.

'Why do you want to know?'

She ignored the question, smiled. 'Why don't you come by the trailer in about ten minutes?'

They were alone and so remote had she become, so unattainable, that the boy looked at her and said, 'Why?'

'If I have to tell you, don't come.' She turned to leave the stage.

'But Taylor—'

She stopped again, looked at the boy. 'We ain't talking about him. There's him and there's me and we're talking about me. You're worried about him, stay the hell away.'

There was nothing that could have kept him away — not a thing in the world.

He didn't wait the ten minutes but was at the trailer door when she came from the kootch tent, caught in the hot night, caught in lust, caught in a curiosity so intense, an anticipation so agonizing, so driven, he thought he would explode and die before she came to the trailer and took him inside.

Her world, her life, were there in the small camper lit by a flyspecked bulb. A make-up table at one end, a bed at the other.

He stared at the bed.

She never said a word. With one hand she guided him to the bed and with the other unzipped his jeans and then she was on the bed and he was with her, on her, in her, around her, trying to do and be all the things he had heard about in all the pool halls and all the bowling alleys and all the school hallways, in all the tall tales and lies told by all the boys who would be men.

It was all of time in the trailer, all of all the time there was.

'Once for you,' Ruby said, smiling and helping him rush, rush though never in such a hurry, never wanting something to start and never never end. 'And once for me …'

It was the once for Ruby that lived, lives for ever. The first to make him hurry and not believe and scream and, with corded neck almost *die* – the first to end for ever his boyhood and give him wonder the rest of life.

But the second to remember, to remember all the big and little things outside and inside. A lamp in the shape of a palomino pony next to the narrow bed with the pink spread and glamour magazines (did any woman ever need them less?) scattered along a crude shelf on the wall and an old pair of drum majorette's boots with tassels in a corner and beer cans on windowsills with lipstick round the punched holes and a table with a round mirror stacked and covered with jars of cream and beauty ointments and oils and feminine mysteries and a clock set in the belly of a ceramic black panther with the hands stuck at 9.20 and clothing draped over books and chairs, clothing that rode next to *her* skin, *her* body, and cheap wood panelling on the walls and ceiling and the light from the carnival filtering through tired shades over slatted windows cranked up to let in all the noise, music, screaming, pulsing *noise*, of the midway while sinking into the wetness, the forever-warm wetness of Ruby.

Ruby.

EPILOGUE

The recruiter sat like a smug pimp.

'You're seventeen?'

The boy nodded.

'And these are your parents' or guardians' signatures stating they'll allow you to enlist in the United States Army?'

Another nod. This time the lie didn't show through the nod and the boy didn't think it would matter anyway. They'd taken a boy he knew who couldn't read and another he knew who was given the choice between the army and prison. How fussy could they be?

The recruiter studied him. He was a sergeant. Impossibly neat. Impossibly clean.

'What branch?'

'I don't know what you mean. I thought I was enlisting in the army.'

'Yes, but *in* the army there are the cavalry and the artillery and the signal corps and the infantry. Which one do you want?'

The boy shrugged. 'I don't know.'

The tight smile, the pimp smile. 'Can you

shoot a rifle?'

'Yes.'

'Good. I'll put you down for the infantry. That's the best branch – all the promotions go for the infantry.'

'Fine.'

'You'll like the infantry.'

'Fine.'

'It'll do you a world of good.'

ABOUT THE AUTHOR

Gary Paulsen grew up in the Philippines and has worked as a sailor, archer, trapper, singer, actor and carnival worker, amongst others. He is the author of many critically acclaimed books for young people, and has won the prestigious Newbery Honor Award three times, for his books *The Winter Room*, *Hatchet* and *Dogsong*. He lives in New Mexico and on a boat in the Pacific, with his wife, the painter Ruth Wright Paulsen.

THE LEAP

BY

JONATHAN STROUD

He fell without a sound, and the waters of the mill pool closed over him. I sprang to my feet with a cry and leaned out over the edge, scanning the surface. No bubbles rose. There was one swirl of a wave, just one, and then the surface was still again, as calm as ever.

No one believes Charlie when she tells them what happened to Max at the Mill Pool. The doctors and her mother think she is in shock; even her sympathetic brother James cannot begin to understand.

So as she recovers in the hospital bed, Charlie vows to hunt for Max alone. She knows that Max is out there somewhere. And to catch up with him, she'll follow his trail wherever it goes – even beyond the limits of this world. And she'll never give up, no matter what the cost.

ISBN 0099402858   **£4.99**

Also by Jonathan Stroud:
Buried Fire ISBN 0099402475   £3.99

Amongst the Hidden

MARGARET HADDIX

All the driveways were empty… And then, out of the corner of his eye, Luke caught a glimpse of something behind one window of the Sports Family's house. A face. A child's face. In a house where two boys already lived.

To the outside world, Luke does not exist. His parents hide their third son away from a society where the penalty for breaking the Population Law is harsh. Then he meets Jen. Suddenly Luke's tiny world is turned upside down.

ISBN 0099402939   £4.99

TURNABOUT

Margaret Haddix

You're going to be able to walk again. You're going to be able to see well again. You're going to be able to hear. I don't know about immortality, but I can promise you this: You're all going to be young again.

What would you do if, on your deathbed, you were offered another chance at life? Selected for Project Turnabout, Melly and Anna Beth are given an injection to reverse the ageing process. At first the results are astonishing, but then they discover that the follow-up shot, designed to halt the process, has proved fatal to all who have taken it.

Now teenagers - and growing younger by the day – they need to find someone to take care of them. But whom can they trust?

ISBN 0099427087 £4.99

I Capture the Castle

DODIE SMITH

As they came toward the barn, I heard them talking. Neil said: 'Gosh, Simon, you're lucky to get away with your life.'
'Extraordinary, wasn't it?' said Simon. 'She didn't give that impression at all last night . . . and they obviously haven't a cent. I suppose one can't blame the poor girl.'

This is the journal of Cassandra Mortmain; an extraordinary account of life with her equally extraordinary family. First, there is her eccentric father. Then there is her sister, Rose - beautiful, vain and bored - and her stepmother, Topaz, an artist's model who likes to commune with nature. Finally, there is Stephen, dazzlingly handsome and hopelessly in love with Cassandra.

In the cold and crumbling castle which is their home, Cassandra records events with characteristic honesty, as she tries to come to terms with her own feelings. The result is both marvellously funny and genuinely moving.

'This book has one of the most charismatic narrators I've ever met.'
J.K. Rowling, author of the Harry Potter books

ISBN 0099845008   £5.99

aidan
chambers

POSTCARDS FROM
NO MAN'S LAND

In a richly layered novel, spanning fifty years, Aidan Chambers powerfully evokes the atmosphere of war while brilliantly inter-weaving Jacob's exploration of new relationships in contemporary Amsterdam.

Jacob Todd, abroad on his own for the first time, arrives in Amsterdam for the commemoration of the Battle of Arnhem, where his grandfather fought fifty years before. There, Geertrui Wesseling, now a terminally ill old lady, tells an extraordinary story of love and betrayal which links Jacob with her own Dutch family in a way he never suspected and which leads him to question his place in the world.

'A superbly crafted, intensely moving novel' SUNDAY TELEGRAPH

'Emotive and thought-provoking' THE BOOKSELLER

'...the type of serious teenage fiction that should be cherished' THE INDEPENDENT

'Writing and literature at its best' SCHOOL LIBRARIAN

'Remarkable for ... clear-eyed self-reflection that also characterises **The Diary of Anne Frank** and the Rembrandt portraits which Jacob so admires' TES

'A terrific novel' DAILY TELEGRAPH

Winner of the 1999 Carnegie medal
Winner of the 1999 Stockport Book Award

ISBN 0099408627   £4.99